It Happened By Design

© 2008 Kathie M. Thomas

It Happened By Design

by Kathie M. Thomas

National Library of Australia Cataloguing-in-Publication Data
Thomas, Kathie M.
It Happened By Design
1st ed.
ISBN 9780975728567 (pbk.).
1. Coincidence. 2. God-incidence.
3. Fate. 4. Plan for life.

Cover design by Jodi Salisbury

Printer: Kingston Digital, 417 Warrigal Road, Cheltenham, Victoria, Australia, 3192. Ph: +613 9555 7733

Bible text: New International Version by International Bible Society

Published by Kathie M. Thomas 2008

What Others Are Saying...

It Happened by Design contains story after story that illustrate the fact that God is always working. This book is eye-opening and will train you to be more aware of God's great love for you as He orchestrates the events of your life in a way that only He can. As you ponder the stories in *It Happened by Design,* you will learn to see God's fingerprints in every aspect of your life. Prepare to be encouraged!

Rebecca Livermore, Author, Speaker, and Entrepreneur.

* * * * *

From the *Foreword,* to the last word of the last chapter, Kathie Thomas's latest book, *It Happened by Design,* captured my attention. I did not stop until I had read the entire book, front to back. The author's writing style, combined with real-life stories, bring the pages to life. As the contributors told their stories about things that had happened in their lives that some might call coincidences, but Thomas calls God-incidences, I was reminded of God's love for each of us, and how nothing happens by accident. It's all part of His plan. The book captivated my heart, and lifted my spirits. Thomas writes from her heart, and her words inspire the reader to be a better person.

Pamela Archer, President
Archer Fitness Consultants, Inc.
http://www.archerfitpress.wordpress.com

$*\ *\ *\ *\ *$

After reading 'Worth More Than Rubies', I just knew I had to read Kathie Thomas's next book *'It Happened By Design'*. *'It Happened By Design'* is about God-incidences and I truly believe that this is what drew me to offer to read and review this book! The stories and lessons related by the contributors are inspiring and eye opening to say the least. I needed to hear the stories within to truly appreciate the wondrous gift I have been given.

'It Happened By Design' shows you another way to view the little things that happen in your life that you may consider a coincidence. Like needing $5 to pay for lunch and finding it in the bottom of your handbag. These aren't coincidences - these are God-incidences. He is showing you his love and support in small, but important ways.

Whilst you can choose to read *'It Happened By Design'* from cover to cover, I recommend that you let Him guide you to the story you need to read. Pick up the book, and just let it open and read the story related on those pages and hear the lesson they relate. That is the power of the stories related within the pages of this marvelous book.

We've all heard of the Law Of Attraction - well God-incidences are the true manifestations of this law. When you believe, and trust that He will provide - He will. My husband and I have always believed that if we trust in a power greater than ourselves - then all will be well. It was so nice to see that others believe and are rewarded in the same manner.

Kathie Thomas has done it again.... *'It Happened By Design'* is an excellent read and incredibly motivational. Well done Kathie and Thank You for another great book.

Charly Leetham, Canberra, Australia
Helping Solopeneurs and Small Business Get
Their Business Online...
http://askcharlyleetham.com

* * * * *

Have you ever experienced an amazing coincidence in your life? One so amazing that later you ask yourself if perhaps it was the hand of God at work? Well, according to author Kathie Thomas, it just might be. She says that instead of a coincidence, you may have experienced a God– incidence.

Kathie first heard the term "God-incidence" from her pastor a few years ago While listening to a sermon on how God used Joseph and his betrayal by his brothers to ultimately save the Hebrew nation, and how everything – every "coincidence" that occurred in Joseph's life -actually moved him closer to his destined path, she realized that she too had experienced many such moments in her own life.

Kathie began searching the internet and found that many others were also having these same experiences. She asked others to share their stories. Those stories became a book – "It Happened by Design".

It's a wonderful book. Kathie has changed nothing in the retelling of the many stories sent to her. They ring with faith and truth. And as you read you realize that, just as Kathie says, the hand of God is moving in the lives of these individuals.

My favorite story is almost the last one in the book – Surprise! God-incidence. It tells the story of a woman who discovers God's calling for her in a surprising way. As I read it, I felt tears come – and then an amazing peace. You see, I have been feeling a similar call as the one in the story – a call to reach out and bring God's word to other women. But then I turn away. Surely God has another plan for a simple business woman from Arkansas? Then suddenly Kathie asks for friends to review her newest book. And I say I will – although I have never done such a thing before. And I read a story of a woman who hears God's call and I know that this is the path I am to take. Coincidence? Of course not! God-incidence! As Kathie shows so beautifully in her book – it happened by design.

Melodieann Whiteley, WealthTogether, Inc.

Table of Contents

Foreword

Coincidences! Have you ever had one happen to you? If so, do you believe it was just luck or random chance, or do you believe it could be something greater?

My father-in-law says a coincidence is when God performs a miracle but desires to remain anonymous! I think he has great wisdom and insight. God performed such a miracle for me recently...

In preparation for bringing our beautiful new baby, Trinity, home from hospital, I had booked my car into an infant car seat fitting service. I drove to the site at the specified time and had our two trusty old car seats with me. While the seat was being fitted I went into the store to pick up a few things that we needed for the baby. A few minutes later the fitter came up to me and told me that one car seat was too old and that the other one was okay but the stabilizer bar was missing and so he couldn't fit it. My heart sank as I was now in a position of having to buy two new car seats – and they aren't cheap! It was going to cost me the best part of $1,000 which I hadn't budgeted for.

With a heavy heart I began looking at new seats and had just about decided on the one I would buy first when the fitter returned. He was amazed that when he had returned to his van and moved something, lying in his van was the exact stabilizer bar to fit my car seat! He couldn't believe it – what luck he said! I was greatly blessed as I had just been saved from spending several hundred dollars.

Was it luck? Was it a coincidence? I think not. I believe it was a God-incidence where He performed a miracle of provision for me just because He loves me!

This is just one example of many I have experienced over the years. I believe in a God who *"sends rain on the righteous and the unrighteous."* In other words, God is looking for opportunities to do you good.

Are your eyes opened to God-incidences or do you put things down to luck or coincidence? It's my prayer that as you read this book your eyes will be opened to see the activity of a loving God in your world on a regular basis. May the journey begin!

Ps Rob Buckingham
Senior Pastor, Bayside Church, Cheltenham, Victoria, Australia

Pastor Rob Buckingham is 50 and is married to Christie. They have three daughters, Georgia-Grace, Paris and Trinity.

Rob is the Senior Minister at Bayside Church - a large, contemporary church in the southern bayside region of Melbourne. Rob started the church in 1992 with a team of 40 people and over the past 15 years the church has grown to about 1,400 people.

Bayside Church is a Christian City Church and Rob is their Victorian State Director. Bayside Church has a strong commitment to make a positive difference in its community and beyond.

As well as his church work, Rob is a well-respected part of Melbourne's media community having worked as an announcer with 3MP for 15 years.

In December 2002 he began working with Melbourne's new Christian radio station, Light FM, where he works part time as their Music Consultant.

Acknowledgements

The stories on these pages are true accounts of events experienced by their authors. Apart from editing for spelling and formatting, the stories have been left as they were submitted to me.

I want to thank all those who contributed stories, ideas and suggestions and their support as I began the journey of writing and publishing this book. A special mention to Meredith who contributed as my proofreader.

A special thank you to Ps Rob Buckingham who is the Senior Pastor of the church I attend. He and his wife, Christie, and the rest of the pastoral team are great encouragers who love to see the church spreading far beyond our building walls.

Thank you also to my daughter, Christine, who is making her debut as a published author in this book. I am excited she had a story to share and I encourage you to watch her blog for announcements of her own book in the not too distant future. I am a very proud mum!

Finally, I want to thank my husband Graham, who is my constant sounding board and encourager. Without his support and being there when I need him, I wouldn't achieve half as much as I do. We all need someone stable in our lives and when that special person is a child of God's too, it makes for a much richer and fulfilling life.

I hope you find these stories give you a reason to start looking for the God-incidences in your own life. If you have stories of your own to share you are welcome to submit them to my blog at **www.god-incidence.com** or visit the website for this book at **www.ithappenedbydesign.com**. Who knows? If I get enough stories, there could be a second edition!

Introduction

It happened by design

I was listening to my Pastor in church late 2005. He was telling the story of Joseph's betrayal by his brothers, and how God had meant everything that happened to Joseph for good. Each person who met up with Joseph, and each circumstance he found himself in, brought him into contact with intended consequences.

Ps Rob used the word 'God-incidence' and it appealed to me. I'd never heard of it before but it was a very apt description of something that could be interpreted by man as a coincidence, but in actual fact was a God-incidence.

I wrote the word down on the sermon sheet in front of me thinking I could weave it into a story somewhere and submit it to a Christian magazine or online publication. Blogging was still a new phenomenon to me at that time but, by the end of the sermon, I realized I had more than one story in me – all factual events that had taken place in my life. When I returned home that day I purchased the domain name 'god-incidence.com', set up a new web space, installed Wordpress software and was on my way.

Imagine my surprise when I did a search on Google only to find that the term 'god-incidence' was not quite so new and was often used. I found that many others wrote about their life experiences too, often using these words and then not long after I began my blog I was contacted by a couple in the US who had seen my blog and were preparing to publish a book about God-incidences. I listed their book on my blog.

In a world where so much bad is reported by the media, fills our newspapers and television reports and shows, it's no wonder that people crave for good news stories – not just stories – but real life events that have happened to others, in order to give them, the reader, renewed hope for their own lives.

It is my hope and prayer that as you read through this book your own hope for your life will be renewed and perhaps you will even begin to recollect incidences in your own life that truly show God has touched you. If that is the case, I would love to know about it as I'm sure that the incidences within are not the end of this story by any means.

For as long as we breathe and remain on this earth, God will always be involved in our lives, whether we realise it at the time or not. Sometimes it's not till the 'punch line' occurs that we look up, or look back, and see His guiding hand upon our lives.

In looking back we begin to realise that what took place was not a coincidence at all because through God *'it happened by design'* – His design.

How this book is organized

The sections of this book have been sorted alphabetically so there isn't any meaning that should be read into what order the sections are placed. The categories covered here are:

Business
Proverbs 3:13 *"Blessed is the man who finds wisdom, the man who gains understanding."*

Family
1 John 3:1 *"How great is the love the Father has lavished on us, that we should be called children of God! And that is what we are! The reason the world does not know us is that it did not know him."*

Finances
Deuteronomy 8:18 *"Remember the Lord your God, for it is He who gives you the ability to produce wealth."*

Health
1 Corinthians 6:19, 20 *"Your body is the temple of the Holy Ghost therefore glorify God in your body."*

Life and God Cares About You
1 Peter 1:7 *"These have come so that your faith—of greater worth than gold, which perishes even though refined by fire—may be proved genuine and may result in praise, glory and honor when Jesus Christ is revealed."*

Relationships

1 Peter1:22 *"Now that you have purified yourselves by obeying the truth so that you have sincere love for each other, love one another deeply, from the heart."*

Travel

Psalm 5:11 *"But let all who take refuge in you be glad; let them ever sing for joy. Spread your protection over them, that those who love your name may rejoice in you".*

Work

John 5:17 *"Jesus said to them, "My Father is always at his work to this very day, and I, too, am working."*

Worship

Psalm 100:2 *"Worship the LORD with gladness; come before him with joyful songs."*

Section One

God and Business

Proverbs 3:13 *"Blessed is the man who finds wisdom, the man who gains understanding."*

Online Networking: Instrument of God

By Lonny J. Gulden

Some months ago I started my own recruiting firm.

I have been truly blessed during this time. Recently I received a resume from a software developer I had met through LinkedIn.com. His start up company had just lost their funding.

I had nothing for him at the time. Two hours later, I received an email from a friend describing an open position at his company that was an excellent match for my candidate.

I set up an interview for my candidate the following morning and received a call from him about 45 minutes after he was scheduled to interview. I asked him how it went and he thought it had gone very well but everybody thinks their interview went well so I thought I'd wait and see.

He then went on to tell me that in the first few minutes of the interview he and the hiring manager discovered they had both graduated from a small Catholic high school in Minot, North Dakota. Now let me put this in perspective for readers who are not familiar with this area.

Minot, North Dakota is a city of about 37,000 residents, making it the fourth largest city in North Dakota, a state with a population of under 1,000,000. Minot is 500 miles away from Minneapolis where the client and the candidate both live. Bishop Ryan High's average graduating class size is 50 students.

Now, I can't tell you what the probability of this happening is, but it truly ranks as a God-incidence in my book.

By the way, he was immediately scheduled for a second interview the following week.

*Known in Minneapolis and St Paul, Minnesota, USA as the Chief Connections Officer™, **Lonny Gulden** has over twenty five years of experience in high technology. Lonny's experience includes executive recruiting, selling to Fortune 1000 corporations, developing alternate channel sales models and advising corporations on information technology strategy.*

Business Ministry

By Kathie M. Thomas

I was sharing with a friend on the weekend about how Graham and I came to be at our current church. We'd been talking about the God-Incidence blog before that, and when she heard the story she told me there was another God-incident I should be sharing. I hadn't thought of that in this way but it is true.

We'd been at our previous church for around 10 years, and our girls had grown up during that time. Graham and I had been house church leaders for 8 years, I had been secretary at the church for a couple of years (until a word was spoken over me some months previously by a visiting Pastor saying that God wanted me in the business world and not working in the church office), Graham had been on the business council and we'd also been the Singles Ministry Leaders. So, we were comfortable there and had fit in well.

However, I'd tried to get some business breakfasts and meetings happening - an outreach to business people. These hadn't been successful but I couldn't help feeling that was what I was supposed to be doing.

Over the last couple of years we'd become restless and different things that happened or were said to both of us prompted us to feel it was time to move on. We discussed this feeling of restlessness and what we should do and where would we go?

A couple of business associates of mine were attending Bayside Church and I knew there was a large group of business people there - I couldn't help wondering if that was the place? The feeling was growing that we needed to mix with other Christian business people - there were few in the church we had been attending. We decided to pray about it and perhaps go attend a service the following Sunday.

All that week every business person I met with was a Christian and attended Bayside. Some of them I'd known for a few years but I had no idea - it had not come up in our discussions until that particular week! I met a couple of business people I'd not known before - they also went to Bayside.

I rang my husband and told him 'all roads lead to Bayside'. So we attended that Sunday and on entry were handed the newsletter, sermon notes and a bookmark with a list of goals for 2005. I scanned the list and my eyes quickly picked up an item near the bottom - a goal to establish a business ministry in the church. I knew

21

immediately we had come to our new 'home' church and that is where we are today. A coincidence? I don't think so!

Kathie M. Thomas is an Author, Blogger, Speaker and Virtual Assistant Coach & Trainer. She has been writing since her early teens and has been published in women's magazines, Christian publications, business magazines and online publications. She published the award-winning "Worth More Than Rubies: The Value of a Work at Home Mum" in 2007.

Going Full Circle

By Kathie M. Thomas

Have you ever had that experience when you've known someone for a time, lost touch and then years later you meet up with that person again? It makes you feel like you've come back to where you were all that time ago.

That happened to me in 2006. Twelve years prior in the first year of my business I worked for a man whose office wasn't far from mine. For a while we kept in touch but then I lost track of him - he'd shifted offices but I didn't know where to and he dropped off my mailing list.

Early 2006 I got an email from the Pastor of my church introducing the name of the man who would head the business ministry in our church - it was the same name as the man I provided support for 12 years ago. I knew instantly it had to be the same guy as his name is quite unusual. But I had no idea he was a Christian and he wouldn't have known it of me either. I guess it was just something we didn't talk about then.

We had our first business ministry meeting at my home and Richard and I were able to be re-acquainted and explain to the others there that we had met many years ago. It felt in some ways that

I'd gone full circle and I feel confident that I'll be working with this man again - not for him as in the past, but for God, with him and the others. The others also shared stories that showed all 5 of us had traveled paths that taught us similar lessons and had now brought us all together.

After that morning's meeting I couldn't help feeling excited - a new chapter was birthing in my life and along with it, many of the business people I've dealt with on and off over the years - all of whom had migrated to the same church. I was amazed as I went through the church directory because I thought I only knew a handful of people but there were 23 and all were business connections! God's got something cooking...

It Dawned On Me Last Night....

By Kathie M. Thomas

... that another God-incident had taken place in my life recently. I'm a bit slow to wake up sometimes.

I was reading the book 'Faith & Work: Do They Mix?' by Os Hillman. This is a great book for those who feel that God is leading them to a ministry in the workplace. I know that is where I am supposed to be and have known it for a number of years now. The book truly emphasizes what I'd been feeling and there was increasing excitement building within me as I progressed through this book.

Readers of my God-incidence blog would know that I had become involved in a new ministry that was birthing at our church - a business ministry. The other members and I all had the same knowledge - a calling by God to serve Him in our workplaces. This book emphasized that.

And yet, I would not have known about this book if it hadn't been for a lady who placed a comment on my blog to one of my other posts. She told me about the MarketPlaceLeaders website and to look in the TGIF archives. There I found a daily devotional called 'Today God Is First' which I now receive. And I also saw more of Os Hillman's books and with three on special; I bought all three. I had no idea this movement was sweeping the world and had been for awhile - I just knew what I was supposed to be doing and that God had shifted Graham and me to Bayside Church for that reason.

Amazing - I started to learn about blogs for a client of mine, got hooked and started doing my own, started the God-incidence one because of something our Pastor said in a sermon some months ago, and then via a comment got propelled further along my path towards my goal. God is so amazing!

More...

Further to the story immediately before this, on the weekend I decided to set up a blog that is dedicated to Workplace Ministry and I hope you will go visit and add your thoughts and comments.

The more I read and research about this aspect of ministry the more I know I have found my purpose. And I suspect many others are finding that too - amazing that you can be blind to something for a long time and then when someone points you in the right direction you can start joining up all the dots and see the picture clearly.

Addendum: Today I write on many blogs and help clients establish blogs. It would seem that this was God's intended path for me and is a fantastic way to reach others online – far more than I could on a face-to-face level.

My sincere thanks to Sophia who placed a comment at my post 'Going Full Circle' as that provided the missing link to join up the dots for me.

The Timing Was Right

By Kathie M. Thomas

It might not seem a lot to you, but it is to me. You see, I'd had a bit of a stressful day and had to deal with some authorities about an 'issue' that has been troubling this household.

It seemed like no-one wanted to help us at all, we were kind of stuck between a rock and a hard place. Then I was given one tiny little bit of advice on that particular day which I acted upon and hoped over time it would bear fruit. But it left me feeling exhausted, teary, stressed and not able to focus as well as I normally do during my work day.

Then I got word late that afternoon that I had been nominated 'Member of the Month' with the Christian Business Women's Network online. Of course, the tears started again, but this time it was because God knew I needed lifting up and what a wonderful way for that to happen. So, I just thought I'd share it with you.

Business Networking for Christian Women

The Christian Business Women's Network is a faith-filled business group hosted on Ryze. Our main focus is to pray, share, teach, learn and encourage one another in our business ventures.

As Christian Businesswomen, we should be outshining the entire business community. We have the favor of God! As we build a successful business we are more and more able to build the Kingdom of God! Let's stand by one another and seek the very best always.

Kathie is our CBWN Featured Member for the Month of September 2006. Kathie loves to encourage and provide sound advice. Her presence on the network is a testimony of dedication and a selfless attitude for helping others! Kathie, thank you for being a blessing to the network and to the body of Christ.

Kathie, is the Owner of A Clayton's Secretary, "the first Virtual Assistant Network in the Asia-Pacific region, second in the world so that makes us one of the longest running Virtual Assistant & Home Based Secretary Networks globally."

If you are eligible (female) I encourage you to visit the Christian Business Women's Network and see what is on offer there for you personally.

Section Two

God and Family

1 John 3:1 *"How great is the love the Father has lavished on us, that we should be called children of God! And that is what we are! The reason the world does not know us is that it did not know him."*

Pilgrimage

By Mulled Vine

This weekend we went to IKEA, a furniture store.

If you're a British husband, this four letter word can strike fear into your heart.

Why did we go? Because my youngest daughter needs a new bed and contrary to what you might think, only IKEA seems to have the right beds. In my opinion they have very nice beds at the local Furniture Village 2 miles away, but no, it has to be to IKEA.

Our "local" IKEA is 30 miles away, a part of a huge shopping complex that serves as a Retail Mecca for millions. It provided hours of "fun": queuing on the roads, endless browsing, queuing for a bite to eat, more browsing, queuing at the tills, and finally, with the day mostly over, the long drive home with thousands of fellow shoppers. And then to add insult to injury, there awaits the hours of frustration as I try to assemble my purchases from the very compact flat packs with obscure instructions that seem to be for completely different products!

So why do I regale you with my tale of woe? Because something unusual happened.

In preparation for our pilgrimage and the anticipated purchase of a fine, and dare I say it, unique IKEA bed, I had to put the roof bars on our car and look for our binding straps. I have a wonderful collection of such straps, accumulated over the years because I constantly misplace them and have to buy new ones. Yet, once again, the blessed straps were missing.

I searched "everywhere" in our garage, through heaps and heaps of chaos. Eventually I gave up in disgust, resigned myself to yet another strap purchase, and turned to exit the garage. As I turned, there was an almighty crash behind me as a basket tumbled from the top of one of our chaotic heaps to the ground. I turned around patiently, thanked God for giving me the opportunity to grow, bent to pick the basket up, only to find it full of my missing straps!

Now you would be within your rights to attribute this to blind chance, as improbable as it is, but I would like today to thank my God for the little things in life.

Mulled Vine, author of mulledvine.blogspot.com, has been a follower of Christ for some 20 years. His journey has sometimes been certain, other times full of puzzlement and even doubt, but it has always returned to the feet of the Master with a wry smile, knowing that no one else has the Words of Life.

God Thing

By Tammie Trainham

My uncle has been through a therapy session that I think every warm-blooded American ought to take into consideration. The suggestion was made for him to create a survival kit for those times of overwhelming stress and anxiety. He was told to make a list of possible items that pertain to each of the five senses. His two favorite items that he listed for the sense of taste were sour gummy worms and black liquorice.

While browsing the Cabela's store, my aunt picked up about six candy items to take to the hospital for my uncle. She walked in and presented him with part of his surprise, a package of sour gummy worms and black liquorice. He asked, "Did someone from here call you?" She assured him that they hadn't called and that it was a God-incidence, a.k.a. God thing.

Another God thing happened the following day. My uncle shared the 'rest' of the list of favorites. One of the favorites for the sense of hearing was a duck call. A friend and business associate stopped by the house that morning and mentioned that someone from work wanted to do something special for Leroy. The guy has a talent...making homemade duck calls out of wood and would be starting one for Leroy. Donna and I shot each other a quirky glance and busted out laughing... "dudu dudu"... another God thing!!!

*As the children's pastor for a co-op of small churches in a farming community, **Tammie Trainham** is known for her unique and insightful lessons. Her stories are great examples of weaving life and lessons into powerful revelations. Over the years, she has written numerous children's stories and modern parables. She relates everyday tasks and observations into Biblical truths. Known as the village "pied piper", Tammie's self proclaimed calling in life is..."to introduce, reproduce, and represent Father, Son and Spirit to kids."*
www.icjesusnu.blogspot.com

"Hope"

By Virginia O'Gorman

This journey begins with my mother, Susanne who was brought up in a rather poor and negative environment. Diagnosed with schizophrenia, she eventually found herself placed in Larrundel, a mental institution. Tragically, at the age of 35 she was found in the grounds of this institution in a case of murder or suicide.

I was her first child whom she gave up for adoption at 2 weeks of age.

Shortly after she gave birth to me as a single mum, she gave me up for adoption knowing that she could not look after me properly. She also decided not to let my natural father, Ernie, be a part of my life. She told him after I had been adopted that he was not ready to be a father.

I was placed in a home where I was the only child for a few years until my little sister Rebecca came along. My adoptive mother, Maureen could not conceive and desperately wanted children, so my adoptive parents applied for adoption and were accepted.

Rebecca was the curious one wanting to know about her natural parents and couldn't wait until the "legal" age where she could find out some more. I, on the other hand, never really cared, or so it seemed, until I reached around 27. The fact that my 20s had been a very unhappy time in my life, probably contributed to finding "my roots" at this age.

In the year of 1994, I decided to go searching. I met the Department of Human Services Worker in a park near where I worked. It was a sunny day and I was very nervous and excited. We sat down on a park bench as the worker unfolded the news that my natural mother Suzanne had been found dead in the grounds of Larundell, as a suspected suicide.

Oh, how my heart sank. I was in shock. I had pinned all my hopes on meeting my mother, and now that was not to be. However upsetting this was, I knew there was nothing I could do. So all I had to do was to get on with my life. My mother had not put my father's name on my birth certificate, so I didn't even have a father to follow up. For me that was the end of that.

However, it was not the end. I was still able to contact the father of my half sister, Linda. My mother had married a man named Jack after giving me up for adoption, and they had a child,

Linda. Meeting with Linda and Jack was a very moving experience. We spent many hours sharing.

Now as for my natural father, Ernie, I thought the search had ended. However, God had a different plan.

I sensed Jesus calling me into a relationship with him in the year of 1996. A few years down the track I was completing a healing course at one of the churches I went to. Whilst completing that course, I received a letter from the Department of Human Services stating that they had more information about my adoption and I needed to contact them.

When I rang them up, they told me that my natural father was looking for me!!! "What?" I thought, "how can this be?" What a miracle! I couldn't believe that my natural father was LOOKING for me.

I'll never forget our meeting. We met at the Stamford Hotel and spent about 4-5 hours there. What a long afternoon. You can't imagine the emotional context of these meetings – you come away feeling exhausted, yet exhilarated! And we have kept in touch ever since. I feel a very special bond with Ernie and have been warmly welcomed by his wife.

The Lord has restored so many things to my life, my soul and spirit, in addition to giving me another father, step mother, some half sisters and brothers, in whom it has been a privilege to get to know.

I have also travelled to Africa to help build a house for orphaned children and my sister and her husband are in the process of adopting 2 children from Africa! It has been an amazing turn around coming from a sense of purposelessness to a journey of faith, love, hope and adventure all because of Jesus!

Virginia O'Gorman is a Christian author who lives in Melbourne, Australia.

Section Three

God and Finances

> Deuteronomy 8:18 *"Remember the Lord your God, for it is He who gives you the ability to produce wealth."*

For Sale

By Mavis Mathews

We were back from Red Lodge and home in Rimini before Christmas. By the end of January our car had died in the driveway, and Ronald was walking the seven miles to the highway and then hitching a ride to town to look for work.

One morning he was cleaning a gun to take to town and sell for grocery money. It was freezing cold and there was snow everywhere. We had just counted our money, one dollar and sixty three cents. But we did not have any unpaid bills or debts except for the home loan from Uncle Bob and Aunt Tatty. We had a little canned milk for the baby and some cans of Campbell's soup between us and starvation. There was a knock at the door.

A nice car was parked in front of our house in this out-of-the-way Montana ghost town, and an older man was tipping his hat to me. "Good morning, ma'am," he said. "We're wondering if this place is for sale?"

When I recovered from the shock, I told him that I would get my husband. My husband came up with a price of $3500, and the couple said they'd take it. It was cash up front. A few days later we sent Uncle Bob his money and boarded a train for California with nothing but our suitcases, leaving the Burbidge place fully furnished just the way we had found it.

Mavis Mathews, an Oklahoma farmer's daughter, tells her story in 'Getting Lucky at Eighty'. It is an inspirational spiritual love affair available where books are sold and at www.gettingluckyateighty.com

Go God!

By Tammie Trainham

At church Miss Peggy shared a testimony that blessed our socks off! Miss Peggy was laid off from her job a month or so ago and the thought of giving $50 bills for birthday gifts to two grandkids was weighing heavy on her heart.

The birthdays were right around the corner and she was praying for a miracle to appear right around the corner (literally). As she went on her walk that day, her route weaved through the neighborhood right past the park. Her prayer that day, 'when I walk by the park, Lord, let me find a hundred dollar bill'. No miracle on 13th Street that day! The next day she prayed again, 'Lord, let me find a hundred dollar bill at the park'. Corners came and went and no miracle on 13th or Cisco Street that day, either.

Then the unimaginable became imaginable. While searching for a receipt in her purse, practically turning it inside out, she gasped. In a zipper pocket, rarely used, there it was... A HUNDRED DOLLAR BILL!!! It just so happened that the remainder of her December 15th Christmas bonus was exactly one hundred dollars and hidden snuggly away for a rainy day!

Tithing Is A Bargain!

By Ian Plumb

Back in 1993 the pastor of our church gave a short series of sermons on tithing. It began with an Old Testament study, moved into the New Testament, and ended with a look at what you could expect from God in a practical sense if you committed yourself to tithing.

I wasn't tithing at the time - while I contributed financially to the church it wasn't a deliberate, periodic tithe. Inconveniently, or so I thought at the time, it came at a period in my life when I had no free cash at all.

At the time I was doing what I could to minimize financial outlays. I was sharing a unit with a non-Christian and a friend of mine was helping me reign in my spending. The budget was tight, to say the least. Yet I had been challenged by these sermons and I knew that I wanted God to be wholly in charge of my finances. So I decided that I would tithe.

I went to my budget-conscious friend and told her of this new expense. We looked at the budget and worked out that I couldn't really afford a complete tithe - only a quarter of a tithe in fact. So I decided that rather than contribute a bit each week I would tithe correctly for one week and not tithe at all for the other three weeks. I simply felt in my heart that this was better than tithing a wrong amount all four weeks.

The big day came when I'd saved up enough to tithe correctly for that week. I felt such a sense of achievement as I dropped the envelope into the offering bucket! I then prayed, explaining to God that I understood tithing, that I appreciated its purpose, and that I really wanted Him to look after my finances.

When I got home that afternoon I discovered that our unit had been broken into. The burglars had smashed the window to my bedroom in order to gain entrance to the property. I called the police and I must admit I was somewhat shocked by the whole incident.

The police arrived in due course and had a look around. There wasn't much to see (and with two young guys sharing a unit it was hard to tell what was general mess and what was a result of the burglary). Then the policeman handed me a form and asked me to list what was missing. I no doubt looked a bit confused so he suggested I just take it a room at a time, listing things on the form as I went round.

There were only four rooms in the unit so the sensible approach didn't take long. As I looked down the completed form I realised that nothing of mine had been taken. Not one thing. Tithing is a bargain - always has been and always will be!

Ian Plumb became a Christian as a young adult, some twenty-odd years ago. These days he and his wife run a school holiday program in Melbourne, Australia, called Kraftworks for kids. He never imagined he would do such a thing – let alone love doing it!

When God Pays The Bill

By Kathie M. Thomas

I had a beautiful son who stayed with us for six months.

One night, I went to see why he hadn't woken for his meal. My son had died. I was later to find out it was cot death. I couldn't understand why it happened - he was my first child, what had I done wrong?

Some of those questions were answered a few years later, but the point to my story at this time is that we were broke, we had little money and we didn't know how we were going to pay for his funeral.

We didn't tell anyone, not even our families, but we did wonder how. I prayed about it, as I do anytime I'm in need. Some family members gave us money to help us (remember though, we hadn't told them).

Without our knowledge, our neighbors took up a collection throughout the whole street. The sums of money given us equaled exactly the quote we'd been given for the cost of the funeral. They didn't know our need either.

When we arrived at the parlor to pay the bill, it seemed that the quotation was slightly out - by $5.00. That was the exact amount I had in my purse! God had provided for us to the exact dollar!

Section Four

God and Health

1 Corinthians 6:19, 20 *"Your body is the temple of the Holy Ghost therefore glorify God in your body."*

God's Protection

By Dale H. Clifton

Two incidences.

First, when I was a teenager, I was trying to impress and scare my date. I was driving at a high rate of speed at night with the lights turned off. I entered a gate and started driving around a huge pile of gravel. I heard a clear voice say, "Stop the car." I slammed on the brakes, turned on the lights and couldn't see a thing in front of the car.

My lights shone into oblivion. There was no reflection. I got out with a flashlight and walked slowly. About ten more feet there was a drop-off. The next day I came back to see what I couldn't see the night before.

It was a 300 foot drop into a stone quarry.

- - - - -

Several years ago at age 61, I evidently (because I do not recall the events myself) started to drive erratically. My wife, Connie, and grandson were with me. I drove down into a ditch and Connie asked me what I was doing? She told me to turn off the key, but I refused. I was driving slow enough that she was able to get out of the back seat and run around the car, reach in and turn the key off.

An off-duty nurse stopped and told Connie that I was having a stroke. A cop approached and asked if I usually drove in the ditch. The nurse told him what was happening. He hollered to the fire station which was just across the road. They sent first responders and an ambulance. At the hospital the best neuro-surgeon just happened to be there to get stuff from his locker. He ordered an MRI.

He asked my wife to come into the "Quiet Room" and told her that based on the MRI I had a very large blood clot, my chances of survival were very, very slim, but that he had already started treatment. If I survived, I would need months and months of rehab. I got a male nurse who had 20 years' experience working with stroke victims. He moved my limbs all night long. I regained consciousness the next morning and walked out of that hospital 24 hours later. A number of the staff came to see me leave. They all said it was a miracle. Three men came into the hospital with strokes that day. I was the only one to leave alive.

The miracle was that everything fell into place and the time from ditch to the emergency room was about 8 minutes. There just happened to be the best doctor in the city there who prescribed the right treatment of which I understand there were 3 choices, and I had the best nurse possible.

I went through NO REHAB.

Dale Clifton, author of The Best Little Scholarship Book in the World, has appeared on ABC, NBC, CBS, Fox and TBN affiliates. Dale says that almost any student can win scholarships, when he/she knows six simple steps. He can be contacted at 1-765-296-4600 or dale@scholarshipdoctor.com

Pray For This Lady!

By Janet Camilleri

One Sunday morning recently I sensed the Spirit of God so strongly it was all I could do to stop myself from standing up and shouting it from the rooftop!

As the pastor led the altar call, God "showed" me an older lady sitting on the other side of the church (I couldn't even see her from where I was sitting!), and I knew she wanted to respond but was holding back.

I didn't quite know what to do – should I say something? But I felt to just stay seated, and to pray fervently for her. Several minutes later, guess who went out the front for prayer and salvation? That was soooo cool!

*For over 10 years, **Janet Camilleri** has been the Editor of "Footprints" magazine for Australian Christian Women. She regularly speaks at women's events, and is the author of "Clues to Your Calling" and "Decadence: Treat yourself to 10 years of Footprints". Visit www.footprints.com.au for more.*

Brain Tumor

By Brenda Ivie

In 1985, my wonderful, dear Daddy was diagnosed with a brain tumor. By the time the doctors realized that his symptoms were not connected to any of the diseases, viruses, drugs, etc. that he had been tested for, the MRI showed a massive tumor growing between the two halves of his brain. It was the size of a baseball and was putting so much pressure on his brain that he could not talk. You could tell by the look in his eyes that he knew what he wanted to say, but it wouldn't come out of his mouth; very, very frustrating for him. He was scheduled for surgery immediately after the tumor was identified.

The morning we were to take him to the hospital, I was in the room when he got out of bed. He reached out for his robe, when suddenly he wet himself. I could tell by his face that it was as much a surprise to him as it was to me and my Mom. I hugged him and said, "Don't worry, when they get that thing out, this won't happen any more. He nodded with tears in his eyes.

After 10 hours of surgery, the doctors came out to us and said they had been able to get the entire tumor out. It had not invaded any of the brain tissue, it was just sitting between the two halves, and it was not malignant. But they also warned us that Daddy had experienced a seizure while on the operating table, which could mean that he may have occasional seizures for years to come, or for the rest of his life. He would have to take medication to control them.

That evening, after he was out of the recovery room, he was able to speak to us, was up walking around and seemed to be doing well. I was praising God for granting the miracle I had prayed for so earnestly. But as the evening wore on, Daddy began to exhibit some strange behaviors. Every few minutes, he would get out of his bed, walk to the sink, turn the water on, and stand there playing with the water for a long time. After a while, I noticed that his head seemed larger underneath his bandages. I went to the nurses' station down the hall and told his nurse what I had been observing.

The nurse came to check on him and told us that there was swelling in the brain and if it didn't subside on its own, he would have to have surgery again, possibly to put in a shunt. After she left, I went downstairs to the small hospital chapel. There was no one else there. I chose a corner where I would not be in anyone's way should someone come in, and I lay down on the floor, on my face and I prayed, asking God to lay His healing hands on Daddy. I also asked that if there were going to be after-effects of the surgery, if He would please be sure they would be something that my Daddy could handle.

The following morning, when Mom and I arrived at Daddy's room, his surgeon was there already examining him.

"The nurse reported that he had some swelling last night. That could have been very serious. But I've examined him this morning and there is no swelling, so he should be fine, now.

Daddy did have occasional seizures for about nine years after his surgery, usually about twice a year. Then, after having a particularly bad one, he ceased to have any more. The only other side-effects he experienced was an erectile dysfunction problem, (my Mom said that he was way ahead of the game anyway), and he still has slow speech. Otherwise, he is a healthy 75 years old, now. God Is Good.

Brenda Ivie lives in tiny Caney, OK, with her husband and three adopted sons, Blaine and Jack, both 15, and Brandt. She is the author of two published novels, and has 8 unpublished novels in the wings. She works for the tribal government of the Choctaw Nation of Oklahoma in the Head Start program.

Doctorese-English Dictionary

By Joanne Sher

The person on the other end of the phone line may not know it, but he is a walking answer to my prayers. I'm in the middle of one of those perfectly orchestrated "coincidences" that only come from God. I am full of questions, and he, it seems, has all the answers.

Knowledge. I have more than I can manage, but still need more. To be more specific, I need information I can actually understand.

Craniotomy. Polycytic astrocytoma. Craniopharyngioma. Optic Glioma. Only a handful of the words I've heard in the past several days, and whose meaning I barely grasp.

I consider myself an intelligent person, with a fairly broad knowledge base. Yet, these medical terms have me baffled. When unknown terms are used in reference to your husband, baffled is not a comfortable place to be.

The neurosurgeon (another word I'd rarely heard, much less thought about, until this week) may be the best, most qualified in the area, but he is no specialist in plain English. I've been given some literature on this assortment of terms, but it was written for Ph.D. candidates. An Internet search was just as fruitless. All I know is that there is some type of mass on Marc's brain, and it's affecting his eyesight.

"What I need is a 'doctorese-English' dictionary." If not, someone who can do the translation for me would surely suffice. Of course, the more knowledgeable this person is about the brain and eyesight, the better. Unfortunately, I'm confident there is no such reference book, and I don't have any friends or family who would qualify as fluent in that particular lingo.

Well, except one - and he's on the phone with me.

Ever since my mother died when I was seven, I have been very close with my uncle Buzzy (her brother) and his wife, Tzippy. They have two daughters, both a few years younger than I am. We girls spent a lot of time together as children.

We soon grew older and started our careers and families in different parts of the country. We didn't stay as close, but still saw each other on occasion. Debbie and Caryn were at my wedding nine years ago, and Marc and I attended Debbie's seven years after that, our newborn son Andrew in tow.

We had met her husband Mark (with a "k") a few times before their wedding (in fact, he'd been Debbie's date to our nuptials), but we didn't know him well. All we knew was he was a friendly, personable guy and he was studying to be a doctor. Now, a bit more than two years after their wedding, my cousin Mark is in his residency somewhere in Texas.

Anyhow, just moments ago I spoke with my uncle Buzzy about Marc's health issues.

"Did you know, Dear, that Debbie's Mark is studying to be an ophthalmologist? I just talked to him about your Marc, and he told me that the doctor he's training under specializes in neuropthalmology (eye function in relation to the brain)."

How's that for a gift from heaven? Needless to say, I got Mark's phone number within minutes. Now, the answer to my prayer is on the other end of the line. The best part is that I actually understand what he's saying. He is speaking in layman's terms about things totally incomprehensible to me not half an hour ago.

Mark has even offered to call the neurosurgeon with specific medical questions and get back to us with the answers. What is better in a stressful situation like this than a knowledgeable, helpful advocate of a cousin on your side?

God is on our side – but we've got both. And some people say these things happen by chance. Don't believe it.

Joanne Sher, *a Christian saved out of Judaism in her 30's, lives in West Michigan with her husband and two children. She is working on her first book, about God's working in her family's life during her husband's serious health issues.*

You can reach her at itsjoanne@chartermi.net or http://joannesher.blogspot.com

Using Scripture for a Healing

By Ethel Ashe-Frear

When I actually became born-again I was part of a weekly Bible class that met in a local home in Damascus, Maryland. I use the term "actually" because for years I thought I was a Christian. After graduating from a Bible College I assumed I was one of those saved people the minister preached about every Sunday morning. Ten years later I found the Holy Spirit and the real meaning of the word "born-again."

One of the teachings at this Bible study was on fasting, beginning with one meal, at least once a week.

Jesus said, "And when you fast, do not put on a sad face as the hypocrites do. They go around with a hungry look so that everyone will see that they are fasting. When you go without food, wash your face and comb your hair, so that others cannot know that you are fasting - only your Father, who is unseen, will know. And your Father, who sees what you do in private, will reward you." (Matthew 6:16-17).

The teaching on fasting is very clear. It is written. Not "if" you fast, but "when"? Another teaching about fasting is written in Matthew 17:19-21.

The disciples said to Jesus, "Why couldn't we drive the demon out?"

Jesus answered, "Only prayer and fasting can drive this kind out; nothing else can."

I remembered the scripture in Luke 11:5-9. Jesus told the following story about a man who did not have any food for a visiting friend. Around midnight he went banging on his neighbor's door.

The neighbor said, "Don't bother me."

The man continued to ask and bang on his door. He was not ashamed to keep asking. Finally the man gave him what he needed.

Jesus tells us, "Everyone who asks will receive, and he who seeks will find, and the door will be opened to him who knocks."

A promise for you written in the Bible.

* * *

Years ago, I was employed by Home Services of Montgomery County in Gaithersburg, Maryland. This particular job was listed through an agency and after three months, if all went well, I was to be hired as a full-time employee.

Home Services is one of the government agencies managed by the county and is designated for patients who have been released from Springfield State Hospital. The program helps folks acclimate themselves back into the community. I was given the job title of Administrative Assistant; I was elected to do whatever needed to be accomplished. It was a very demanding job.

This particular Tuesday morning, several of the patients asked if I would show them how to use one of the older software programs, MultiMate. After the session we stopped for lunch. In order to finish up some work I began earlier in the day and it was necessary for me to move a large heavy typewriter to my desk at the other end of the building.

"I've got to get help moving this typewriter," I said to myself.

Of course, there is never anyone around when you really need help. I lifted the typewriter placed it on a chair with wheels and pushed it to my work area lifting it again to my desk.

The next morning while getting dressed for work I experienced pain in the lower part of my back. I did not pay much attention to it at the time. As a runner I was accustomed to a little pain once in a while. Several days later, the pain increased. By the end of the week I was in constant pain and it was difficult to move. I felt like I was being stabbed in the back with a sharp knife. I did not mention it to anyone at work because I thought my job might be in jeopardy.

"There is only one answer," I said. "I need healing and when I begin this fast it's going to take commitment and determination."

I set up my fasting guidelines. I did not eat solid food but drank liquids that contained no calories. I had read many books on this subject; this was my personal way of fasting, it worked for me over the years and I stuck with it.

The first few days of my fast were not too difficult. I'd done this before and knew what to expect. The body wants food and it will continue to remind you of that fact. I was still in constant pain and the pain became so severe I chose to sleep lying on the floor flat on my back.

"Don't roll over," I said out loud.

I tried not to move, movement caused excruciating pain. For one reason or another, I have never been one to take medicine and it never really occurred to me to take an aspirin! I know that might sound like strange thinking, but that's the way it was. I remember the agony of constant pain, coping with my job during the day and trying to sleep at night.

In order to get up off the floor in the morning, I carefully rolled over on my side, moving ever so gently, leaning on my elbow and then pushing up with my hands to a sitting position. I sat for a good five minutes, trying to muster up enough courage to get to my feet. I was determined not to miss any days of work; I still had bills to pay.

I looked up scripture. My resource book was Strong's Concordance and wrote down all the healing verses I could find. When I was not working my eight-hour job, I wrote scripture.

After two weeks of non-stop pain I will never forget this one Monday morning. I rolled over in my usual way in order to get up and heard my back pop in two different places. I didn't think much about it because I was still in pain. By 1:00p.m. that afternoon my pain was gone. It never returned. Fasting combined with the power in the scriptures took effect!

I breathed a quiet prayer. "Thank you Lord for my healing."

I was now sleeping in my comfortable bed. Later that same week getting up to go to work I heard another pop at the base of my spine. I was not aware anything else was "out of place" but God knew. I assumed my running and my heel hitting the pavement many times previously could have put that area of my body out of kilter. I am grateful for that unexpected healing as well.

Scripture: Good News for Modern Man (GNFMM) Thomas Nelson, Inc. 1966

Ethel Ashe-Frear *is a graduate of The Baptist Institute, Bryn Mawr, PA and NRI McGraw-Hill Center for Writing, Washington, D.C. Self-published "Healing Scriptures", 2007 used in local hospital pastoral care ministry. "Germs in Ice?" published in the National Institutes of Health (NIH) Record 1996, as well as many scriptural articles in local hometown newspapers.*

www.helium.com/users/405896

Section Five

God and Life

1 Peter 1:7 *"These have come so that your faith—of greater worth than gold, which perishes even though refined by fire—may be proved genuine and may result in praise, glory and honor when Jesus Christ is revealed."*

The Divine Dream of Light and Love

By Shirley Cheng

One night, I dreamed a dream I can and will never forget. I do not remember exactly how old I was; I was perhaps nine. I do not even recall whether I was in China or America; within my first eleven years of life, my dear mother Juliet Cheng and I went to China six times to seek treatment for my severe juvenile rheumatoid arthritis, so some memories are blurred together between two countries.

The dream was a portrait of a man, a young Caucasian man. It was just like a photograph in the sense that the man never moved or spoke. His eyes were very kind and caring, so if one would meet him, one would instinctively trust him on the spot. His wavy brownish hair framed his face and touched his shoulders. What distinguished this man from any other man was the light that emanated from his entire being. It was a white yellowish light, a soothing light, nothing blinding or piercing. Despite the fact that he was completely engulfed in this light, it did not veil his crystal-clear features.

The photograph-like appearance went away after what seemed like a minute. But it is hard to tell time in dreams.

After waking up, I knew immediately of whom I dreamed, and shared it with my mother.

I dreamed of Jesus Christ, and he was around seventeen. That age was never told to me in my dream, as there was no sound; I simply knew with conviction.

Seventeen was when I lost my eyesight.

After all these years, it sends shivers down my spine just to think that my dream was that of Jehovah God Almighty giving me a message through His beloved Son, the Christ.

Was the divine sign a warning or support? I feel it was both.

Above all, I am terribly honored and humbled that Jesus Christ would appear in my dream. How often could I have such a high honor? It has got to be the best, the most special, and the most stunning, dream I have ever had, and I will always treasure it in my heart as long as my soul is in existence. Whenever I think back to the young Christ in my dream, I instantly feel safe and secure. Yes, I am always being loved, watched, and protected!

Through the years, I know God has been watching over both Mother and me. We have had to climb many steep mountains and cross numerous deep oceans, and His loving Being has always been there, supporting us, guiding us, and loving us.

Thus, neither of us ever feels alone, and it is our deep, unwavering faith in Him that has allowed us to take giant steps forward. For instance, faith in Him had given my mother great stamina and courage to fight for my life during two custody cases. She lost custody of me twice in America only after disagreeing with doctors' recommended treatments - treatments that could have sent me to my grave, or worse, paralyze me. (In America, parents risk losing custody of their children forever if they disagree with doctors' recommended treatments or even when they want a second opinion.) She knew she would win both cases because she found strength in Him and that she had the power of reasons in her hand.

With God and Jesus Christ always in my heart, I remain strong in mind and spirit, and I continually love the life I live even after I lost my eyesight. Think about it: why should I resist all the wonders of life just because negativity decides to bump into me? Compared to the entire universe and all the beauties it contains, my problems are tiny! God gave me my life so I can enjoy it to its fullest, and this is exactly what I will always do. I am simply so honored to be alive; I am so honored that He has chosen me to live, so I want to show Him how much I truly cherish and love the present He gifted me. Because of my life, I am so privileged to know, discover, and experience all the wonderful things life has to offer. I am able to laugh; I am able to weep. Without my existence, I would be able to do none of these.

Having the knowledge that there is a Creator, I know life is not about the worldly aspect but all about the spiritual realm. Suffering on Earth is to strengthen our faith. Challenges and obstacles are exercising machines for your spirit. I believe God has much more prepared for those who can endure the trials and tribulations here, so we can be strong enough to receive an everlasting life of love and happiness under His mighty and just rule. Therefore, I concentrate on the spiritual aspects of life: faith, love, values, hope, gratitude, and many other priceless commodities that everyone needs to embrace. If we only achieve those of the worldly, such as wealth and fame, what we gain will only die along with us. On the other hand, if we welcome a life of love and values, we will leave an enduring legacy.

Although I'm blind, I can see far and wide; even though I'm disabled, I can climb high mountains. Let the ropes of hope in God haul you high!

Shirley Cheng *(b. 1983), is a blind and physically disabled award-winning author with eight books (including Embrace Ultra-Ability! and The Revelation of a Star's Endless Shine), motivational speaker, self-empowerment expert, poet, and contributor of fourteen further books, as well as board member of World Positive Thinkers Club.*

Visit http://www.shirleycheng.com

Look Straight Ahead

By Debra Shiveley Welch

Sitting on the couch in my mother's living room day and night, doing nothing but rocking, rocking, rocking, I was uncertain if I could survive this devastating blow. Unable to eat, I was still having problems with anorexia and the slightest stress would throw me into week-long fasts. I was becoming weak and my already slight frame emaciated. My heart was broken. Once again, I had been thrown over for someone else and my fragile pain-ridden spirit could endure no more.

I am not sure how long I had been living back home with my mother. All I know is that I had not moved from the couch, had not changed my clothes, eaten, or taken any liquids. I was an empty shell and had it not been for what happened next, I don't think I would be here today.

I had lain down on the sofa and closed my eyes. Did I sleep? I must have, because what happened next could only have been a dream.

I found myself on a dirt road. I remember it was hot...and the dust was swirling in places, irritating my nose; I sneezed. I saw a man up ahead, sitting on a bench. I walked over to him slowly as you sometimes walk in dreams… so slowly that it was almost as if I were standing still and he was moving toward me. I stood before him swaying slightly; even in the dream, I was weak from not eating. The man reached up and drew me down onto his lap, pressing my cheek to his shoulder.

The material of his shirt irritated my cheek, but I didn't want to move my head. I felt peaceful and content. I think I may have been ready to die right there, filled with a serenity I had only found in the deep woods and rolling pastures of Southern Ohio.

He began to speak. His voice was deep and resonant, a lot like Robert Duvall's voice; so deep and rich, that it almost sounded like singing, it was so melodious. "I love you," He said, rocking me like a baby. I remember asking, "How will I know this is not a dream?" He answered, "When you awake, look not to the right or left. Do not look behind. Look straight ahead and your answer will be there." When I awoke, there was a cross on the wall directly ahead of me. It remained there until the day we moved, when it disappeared as magically as it had appeared.

Excerpt from Son of My Soul – The Adoption of Christopher, Debra Shiveley Welch, Saga Books: Chapter 9 "The Forgotten."

Welcome Back

By Debra Shiveley Welch

I awoke on the morning of August 2, 1977 with such intense nausea, that I barely made it to the bathroom. You can imagine my horror when upon vomiting I beheld a stream of bright, red blood! The heaving went on unabated. I could not stop it until finally, blind, I surmise by a dramatic drop in blood pressure, I felt my way to the top of the stairs and called for Danny. He found me, unconscious, on the bathroom floor, where I had felt my way back, still blind, to vomit again.

***

There was no tunnel. There was simply this lovely, soft, ever brightening light. It was like being cradled within a frosted light bulb – all white and soft and glowing, and it was as though the air was made up of music and vibrations. It was a place of teaching, a place of learning, a place... of love. Slowly, oh so slowly, I became aware of a feeling of complete acceptance. Here was love!

Profound, exquisite love! I was bathed in it, enveloped in it, completely surrounded by it. I was with God, Creator, whatever name you wish to give the Supreme Being, and I was saturated with love! Finally, I understood what He meant in my earlier vision when He said, "I love you!"

To come to any kind of understanding of what I felt, one would have to go back, back, back to when they were so very young, were hungry, maybe crying. Their mother would come, pick them up, and hold them, and they went from being hungry and uncomfortable to a feeling of warmth and safety and love. That comes as close as I can get to explaining how I felt.

I had never experienced this type of love and acceptance before. I remember thinking, 'this is how it is! I knew it would be this way!' And, I remember finally feeling whole and worthy and safe.

There is a saying that goes something like "Recipe for a happy adult: Take one child, marinate in love for approximately 16 years until ripe and juicy." This must be what God does. We are not aware of it on this plane, but deep down, the love is there. I don't think we could function if we felt the full force of God's love. The glory of it would be too distracting.

When I went home, I recognized it instantly and knew that it had been there all along! Now, I knew who I was! I had my reference, my compass, my oar! I was so happy, so very, very happy.

It was with a great deal of reluctance, that I opened my eyes in the Intensive Care Unit of the hospital. I returned to this life with deep sorrow for what I had left behind. I felt lonely, bereft, robbed of my birthright. I was back in the cold, heartless world in which I had spent 24 years, without love, protection and companionship. I wept.

I felt someone holding my hand and looked up. There was Michelle, a friend of mine, who was a nurse at the hospital. She smiled, and smoothing the hair back from my face, whispered through a tear-filled voice, "We thought we had lost you. Welcome back."

Excerpt from Son of My Soul – The Adoption of Christopher, Debra Shiveley Welch, Saga Books: Chapter 10 "The Reborn".

Born in Columbus, Ohio, award-winning author **Debra Shiveley Welch** *resides in Central Ohio with her husband, Mark and son, Christopher, also an author.*

Author of three books, Debra is currently writing Cedar Woman, *her first romance novel. All are available through www.sababooks.net, Amazon and Barnes & Noble.*

debrawelch@debrashiveleywelch.net

Messages

By Lesley-Anne Evans

Messages surround us. They are audible or inaudible, obvious or subliminal. They wait for us in e-mails and on answering machines. They bombard us from radio and television, newspaper and magazine. They pop up on cell phones like uninvited guests. Messages are everywhere.

And my personal experience suggests that the most profound messages are often those I have to prick up my ears to hear.

I believe that God speaks through us and to us, orchestrating messages and messengers with divine timing. My problem is that I don't always recognize his fingerprints on things, although I do now more often than I used to.

I also used to think that the messages God wanted me to convey were the big and important ones - the mission-sized ones. So I kept searching for those big ideas, becoming quite frustrated when opportunities for great things never presented themselves.

Then a good friend suggested that God might use me to pass on simple messages, too. Like when my response to the pain in another's eyes was a hug. That was God speaking, through me. Or the time I let someone more stressed than me go ahead of me in the grocery line, even though I was also pressed for time. That was God speaking, through me. And there was the time I felt compelled to knock on my neighbor's door, to make sure all was well. That was God speaking, through me, too. The paradox is that, each of these simple messages from God, through me, can have a kingdom-sized impact.

My friend's advice helped me to realize that God's hand can be seen in all things - momentous or not. And that was a revelation.

Years later, I now also understand that the quiet sense of urgency to act is the voice of God speaking into my heart. Although being obedient to that voice is sometimes a struggle, I'm learning to obey it - and thus be God's messenger.

In a similar way, God uses others to speak to me. They offer encouraging, edifying, life-giving words from God's heart to mine. But even here, I'm not as dialled in to these messages as I want to be. Sometimes God needs to knock me over the head to get my attention!

Like the time the phone rang early on a Saturday morning. A dear friend of mine, mother of three and pregnant, called because I was "on her heart", and was obedient to the prompting.

She didn't know that a recent medical test had revealed a suspicious mass on my ovaries. She had no idea of what was going on in my life. God knew. And so God spoke into her heart, and she called me. In her voice I heard an echo of the Father's voice. He used her to touch me in a tangible way. God amazes me!

So as I write this, I smile as I think about God's messages to me that day. My friend phoned to say hello. She wanted me to know she cared, and her message warmed my heart. God blessed me with more. He said, "You are on my heart, Dear One. You matter to me. I am watching you. I know everything about you. I have everything under control. I need you to hear my voice. It's me, dear one. Are you listening?"

I was all ears that day.

Still other seed fell on good soil. It came up and yielded a crop, a hundred times more than was sown. When he said this, he called out, "He who has ears to hear, let him hear." Luke 8:8

Songbird

by Lesley-Anne Evans

Sun breaks through mid-morning.
Your quick movement catches my eye,
single songbird perched on Joe's S.U.V.

You sing, tail bobbing, happy for the day.
Then, suddenly swooping down, you
throw yourself at the mirror.

Again and again you flutter there pecking at the
glass,
frantic in your attempt
to make some narcissistic connection,

or to pass into what looks
better
behind the looking glass.

I stand barefoot in the doorway watching,
dog lounging at my feet,
sun warming my toes.

Joe
was that you this morning,
sharing peace before you passed into something
wonderful?

Did you sing?
Are you singing now?
Did you flutter, caught between
the present and a reflection of glory just beyond
the glass?

And then,
in the blink of an eye, fly
                        ...away?

Lesley-Anne Evans, *University of Guelph, B.L.Arch. 1987*

Lesley-Anne Evans is a freelance writer and poet. She lives, nearby lakes and mountains, in beautiful British Columbia, Canada, with her husband, three children and dog.

Lesley-Anne invites you to join her at www.gracenotes.ca.

Who Are You Walking Past?

By Kathie M. Thomas

I was running later than usual this morning when I went down to the post office to check for mail.

As I walked along the pavement a young lady was walking towards me, her head down, reading the book in her hands. She must have just come off the train - there was a fair bit of foot traffic around. I don't know why I was watching this lady but, as she got closer, I noticed the book was moving up and down with the movement of her walking. And in a flash, as the book moved up momentarily, I saw the cover of her book and my heart jumped!

The book was mine - *"Worth More Than Rubies"*.

I stopped and watched her as she moved further down the road away from me, wondering if she even realized she had just walked past the author.

Probably not.

How cool was that? Definitely a God-incident in my books!

Section Six

God Cares About You

1 Peter 1:7 *"These have come so that your faith—of greater worth than gold, which perishes even though refined by fire—may be proved genuine and may result in praise, glory and honor when Jesus Christ is revealed"*

My Birthday Angel

By Terri Tiffany

I was spending my 52nd birthday alone since my only child married the year before and moved to Seattle. My husband worked, but even still; he hated to shop. Mary (thank Heaven for name tags) made me thankful I had turned a year older.

Shelly called us the month before to announce the news of our first grandchild. I cried myself to sleep that night certain my dreams of living near her were over. Why had I ever sent her to college in the first place? On her first day, she'd met my future son-in-law. Now my grandchild would always know me as the other grandparent.

That morning, my husband kissed the top of my head now securely buried under my covers. "Have a good birthday. I'll see you tonight." I moaned goodbye and forced one eye open. Presents waited for me on the dining room table. My daughter's package had arrived the day before but she warned me not to open it until today.

I peeled back the pink and blue paper. A fuzzy copy of the first ultrasound of the new baby greeted me. My flesh and blood. Not that I could make out head nor tail but seeing the picture of the baby growing in my daughter's belly suddenly made being a grandmother real — a grandmother who couldn't be further away.

My plans to spend the weekend with a good friend prompted me to shop for some new clothes. I hoped the thrill of trying on tops would dull the aching reminder that I was spending my birthday without my daughter for the first time ever. How would I ever get used to having no family near me? After she had shared her news and after I recovered from my weeping fest, I began a prayer journal. My number one prayer: either move me closer to my daughter or make me happy in Florida.

I found it... the perfect blouse to go with the necklace Shelly had sent me. Trying it on, I was pleased with the fit. I worked my way over to the jewellery counter to purchase earrings to match.

"Can I help you find anything?" I shook my head 'no' and moved towards some silver accessories. "Is there anything in particular you're looking for?" One, two, three... I hated pushy sales people, but it was my birthday. I'd be nice. I looked up and discovered a tiny, woman complete with grey hair. Her neck and arms dazzled with jewellery. She selected an odd pair of earrings and brought them closer for my inspection. "I just love this set. What do you think?"

I didn't love them. I finally shared that I needed matching earrings for the shirt I had draped over my arm. She chatted while I looked. "I once met the owner of this store. I was just a teenager and lived in Virginia. He's a Christian man and very old now." She shared some personal history and then asked me how long I had lived in Florida and whether I liked it.

Did I like it? I did when my family was here.

"I'm not sure, you see, my only child married last year and moved to Seattle. She's expecting her first child and I'm so far away." I didn't want to say too much for fear I would bawl in front of a perfect stranger.

"I know exactly what you're going through. I have one child, a girl, and when she married, she moved to Tennessee. When she had her first child, my only grandchild, I was so far away and worried that the child would never know me." She leaned over the counter and I caught a twinkle in her eye.

"Wouldn't you know, I am as close to my granddaughter as I am to my daughter." She smiled and stood straighter. "Honey, distance doesn't have to make a difference... especially if you are a believer. Are you a believer?" I nodded my head. "Then," she continued, "God knows all about how you're feeling and He'll make it right — wherever you are."

We stood together at the jewellery counter in the middle of the busy store as if we had known each other all our lives. Mary had lived a duplicate of my life complete with all the fears and loneliness. Her words reassured me that God understood my pain and he wouldn't forget me.

After we finished our talk, I knew I had been handed the best birthday present ever.

Terri Tiffany *counseled adults for seventeen years before owning a Christian bookstore. She resides now in Florida with her husband where she writes fulltime.*

Her stories have appeared in Sunday school take-home papers, women's magazines and numerous anthologies. Please visit her at http://terri-treasures.blogspot.com.

God is always speaking to you

By Kathie M. Thomas

I recently read how God is always there, always seeking to get our attention, always talking to us, but in the busy-ness of life we tend to overlook this. I'm definitely guilty of that, even when I do respond to promptings by the Holy Spirit to pray for people.

We had been going through a 40 Day Prayer & Fast time at our church. A couple of weeks previous during my prayer and Bible reading time I was prompted to pray for a couple I'd not seen for some years. They used to go to our old church and then shifted to another state to minister at a church there. I knew they'd been having challenges and we'd heard on the grapevine occasionally about things happening in their lives. But we weren't close friends and we hadn't maintained contact.

So, to be prompted to pray for them wasn't because they were always on my mind and I knew it was not of my own thoughts. I prayed for them and that God is with them in whatever is happening currently, and after my prayers for that day got on with my life. They didn't enter my mind again... till the following Sunday. Who should walk into my (new) church that morning but this couple and their children? I had an overwhelming feeling of joy and excitement about seeing them and fired heaps of questions at them: how long have they been back; how are they; where are they living; and so on. I didn't know who to hug first and excitedly chatted to them and then moved off to sit in my usual spot but keeping aware of where they had sat in the auditorium.

The prompting came back within minutes for me to go sit with them and I walked around to see if there was a spare seat near them. There wasn't, so I moved back to my seat and waited for children's church to start as I knew there would then be vacant seats. I grabbed my things and moved over to that side of the building and sat with them.

During the service I was reminded of the prayer and concern for them a couple of weeks ago and I shared it with the husband after the service, with tears filling my eyes. David and I had worked together a few years ago and had some common ground so I felt I could share this with him.

I still don't understand why I was so overwhelmed with emotion for this couple. We'd not been close friends but did know each other. We didn't mix in the same circles and their children are very young - ours are full grown - and yet I know I was prompted to pray for them and then totally excited to see them this morning. They're trying to buy a home and once settled will decide on their new church home.

One more amazing thing in all this, the husband told me he was surfing the web during the week and came across my blog - I asked him which one? I owned 12 at that time. He told me the one about my book, "Worth More Than Rubies", and was thrilled to come across it. He doesn't even know how he found it - so there you have it. God had me thinking about them and vice versa - amazing.

Whatever is happening I know that God was in it, and for them to turn up in the church I attend out of all the churches they could attend, I feel was a God-incident in itself - that coupled with the prompting to pray for them.

A New Year God-Incidence

By Kathie M. Thomas

I almost forgot to share this at my blog but had mentioned it at the Workplace-Ministry blog and emailed some close friends and family members about it.

For several years I have prepared my goals for the year in full color using PowerPoint and then print them out, laminate them and stick them on the wall just above and behind my computer monitor so that whenever I'm looking at my monitor, the goals are also in view. I believe it's important to have our plans and goals constantly in our vision - if they're out of sight, they are often out of mind, and the end of the year can come and we wonder what happened to our plans. It's been important to me that I adopt a Bible verse as well for my goals, and I include that. The goals usually include business goals and personal goals with something that also relates to my ministry and/or my connection with my Christian faith.

Late in December 2006 the pastor from my church told us about the message he received from God for our church and the Year of the Green Lights. I added this information to my PowerPoint poster and the verse he quoted, plus pictures of green traffic lights for emphasis and the word 'Go' in a big green circle.

Mid-January 2007 I had set aside a day for planning the rest of my year and my focus for what I want to do. It's not a coincidence, but a God-incidence that at the very time I was writing and praying about my goals, a Google Alert arrived in my email, with my name in it, promoting a speaking event in the US.

This blew me away - almost like a confirmation that I would be doing a lot more speaking. I had already had several engagements booked for that year - but hadn't yet done a lot to promote, other than change my website (kathiethomas.com) and my email signature block.

The Google Alert just lets me know whenever my name is published on a website so I can track what's happening out there - only this time the Kathie Thomas wasn't me. But just to see my name there with Lisa Bevere's was an exciting thought! And it felt like an encouragement and confirmation. There is a speaker in the US with the same name as me and she was to be sharing the stage with Lisa Bevere. That email so excited me and I copied and pasted it into the PowerPoint poster before I printed it off.

You see, one of my goals for that year was to increase how much writing I do, publish a book and do more speaking engagements. This email which could have come anytime, arrived during the time of my planning session and prayer and I believe it to be a confirmation from God that He is directing my path. And already I've had several articles published, am writing a book based on one of my most successful blogs and have already had several speaking engagements.

Addendum: I achieved around 90% of my written goals in 2007, including completing and publishing a book and speaking at many events. The following year I secured my first international speaking engagement and over 30 other engagements as well as completed this very book you are now reading. Again, my goal sheet for the year was stuck on the wall beside my computer monitor...

Daily Matters

By Kathie M. Thomas

There are things that happen on an almost daily basis that would be seen as a God-incidence if only we were aware of them.

One Thursday early 2006 I was down at my church, helping with a mail out. When it was time to go, I went to say goodbye to Pastor Georgina, but saw she was in the Senior Pastor's office so decided not to interrupt her. I turned to go and both of them called out to me to come back. Both had been reading my articles online and wanted to encourage me as they felt the articles were good. We began chatting and I shared about some recent publishing successes I'd had - writing is one of my passions (you hadn't guessed, had you?).

Ps Georgina and I had been discussing which connect group my husband and I might lead that year. Graham and I still hadn't settled on anything but then Ps Rob said 'why not a writer's group?' and Ps Georgina agreed. The three of us talked excitedly about it for a few minutes before I had to move on but my heart had quickened and the idea was indeed exciting.

The amazing thing though, was just that morning I had been reading about setting up a Christian Writer's Group at the FaithWriters.com website - I'd never looked at that before and I was wondering about it. So to have Ps Rob suggest it and Ps Georgina agree on the very same day I'd been considering it seemed to be another one of those God-incidents for me and I expected it was something that would take place.

Postscript*: The Writer's group certainly did happen and new friendships were formed.*

Right Time, Right Place

By Christine Thomas

January 2006, I traveled to Ireland to complete a five month course studying and working with horses. Previously, I had completed another course that offers a scholarship to this stud in Ireland. I applied for the scholarship, but didn't achieve this.

However, I still believed it was a place I was supposed to go and that I would get a lot out of doing the course. So, I applied outside of the scholarship, deciding I could afford to pay to go. Again, I was knocked back after being informed I was on reserve and if anyone declined their acceptance, I was in line. I was encouraged by mum to see how I could improve this position and make it into the course, so I contacted them and it was suggested I work another year and apply again with updated references.

Over twelve months I gained invaluable experience, applied again and was accepted. As a Christian I am aware that I should be looking for a Church to attend while overseas, but didn't look into this wholeheartedly. There were other things too that I would be missing out on while over there – my guitar, Christian friends, family and people to speak into my life. Silly, but although most of these could be provided through a Church family, I didn't give much thought to looking into one that would be similar to that which I attended at home (an Assemblies of God - AOG) in the country.

I'm definitely not using this as an excuse to just sit around and expect God to provide, but amazingly when I arrived at the stud, the first thing to greet me in my room was a guitar – it belonged to my friendly German roommate. Now if this wasn't enough, one of the other girls who I grew close to also had one and was learning, so we were able to play together and encourage each other.

Coming up to my first weekend off, I was in my room reading my Bible with the door open. One of the girls wandered by and spotted the book. I quickly found out she was a Christian – the only other Christian on my course. She too had the coming weekend off and took me to a Church she had been attending as she had been living in Ireland for some time. The Church – one that just happened to be recognized as an AOG – had an amazing family and we were quickly welcomed in, soon attending young adult services when free and a weekly Bible study.

I have a list of goals for my life and studied French while in high school. Although I hadn't touched on it for a couple of years, I still wanted to visit France and improve my French. The young Christian woman took me and another friend to her home town of Angers in France over a long weekend that she managed to get off for each of us and I was blessed to attend her Church – another AOG – while in the country and meet some of her gorgeous friends.

Following my course, I visited France again for two and a half weeks, staying with the other French girl on the course – the one who had been playing guitar with me. Even interests that aren't needs in my life, but rather wants, God provides for.

Through delaying my attendance at this particular course for a year, He put me in an environment where I was able to have a strong Christian friend, my wants were provided for and many opportunities were given to live out my faith, serve others and encourage them and even witness. Coincidence? I think not.

Christine Thomas has grown up in Australia in a Christian family where she and her sisters have been encouraged to pursue that which they're passionate about. Her desire is to educate those interested in horses and enlighten them to possible careers within the equine industry. You can view her blog at http://equus.thomases.org/

Bringing Comfort

By Jill Ammon Vanderwood

When I woke up, and reluctantly pulled myself out of bed, on a rainy Saturday, in late October, I had no idea the Lord would use me as an instrument to bring comfort. I also had no idea I could help answer the prayer of a young mother.

Our neighbors had moved to the country and invited my family to a house warming. I bundled myself into my purple raincoat and drove to Bed Bath and Beyond to pick up a gift card. I ran from the car to the store and stood in the entryway to take off my wet raincoat. Near the door were several shopping carts with comforters marked $9.99. What a buy. I picked up two blankets encased in plastic and continued to the checkout where I could purchase the gift card.

A family in front of me had several comforters which were blue and brown. But when I came along, there was only one blue, and the rest were two-tone pink.

When the cashier rang up my purchase, the price was $6.99. After taking my purchase out to the car, I returned to the store for more pink comforters, ending up with eight in all; some blankets were full size and some twin size.

The rain continued to pour as I drove to the grocery store, with these bulky blankets filling the front and back seats of my car. While at the grocery store, I met up with a young, single neighbor who had recently moved into her father's home. She told me she had walked to the post office and then to the store. Offering the soaking wet girl a ride home, we stacked the plastic covered bundles into the back seat.

"Do you need a warm blanket for your bed?" I asked the shivering girl. "I bought eight all together and I'm not sure what to do with all of these pink comforters."

"Sure," she said, "If you don't need them."

"This will be your early Christmas gift. What size is your bed? I have twin or full size."

"My bed is full size," she said. "Thank you, thank you so much, for the ride and the blanket."

"I'm so glad I ran into you today," I told her.

"Me too," she said, getting out of the car and hugging the comforter.

I decided to give another blanket to a single, college student in my neighborhood. She, too, chose a full-size. My granddaughters didn't need them, and my grandson has a full-size bed, so he

104

couldn't use the blue comforter. The blue comforter was donated as a raffle for the Wheelchair Foundation.

An offer was made to Sub-for-Santa, at my church. My church leaders said they may have a need for two comforters. Setting those aside and I still had three.

I called my neighbor, Sylvia, who has a daughter with eleven children, knowing most of her children were boys. Sylvia said they can always use blankets, and she could store them until her daughter, Lene, came to visit.

After Christmas, my neighbor asked where I got the blankets. I told about Bed Bath and Beyond's October sale. "But my daughter wants to know how you knew to only buy the pink ones. She also wants to know why you gave her three blankets, one being a full size and two being twin."

I told her, "I only had one blue one and the rest were pink. Everyone who needed a blanket got one, and they picked the size they needed for their own bed. Then I gave your daughter the three pink blankets, I had left."

Sylvia told me, "my daughter's husband is in Iraq. In October, her furnace went out. The boys sleep upstairs where it keeps pretty warm. The girls all sleep in the basement where it can get cold in November and December. A neighbor repaired the furnace as well as her could, but the basement was still cold. Lene got down on her knees and prayed for blankets to keep her girls warm. Right after that, their family visited our home and I sent her home with one full-size and two twin-size, pink blankets. Two girls sleep on a set of bunk beds, the top bunk is a twin bed and the bottom is a full-size bed. The other girl has a twin bed."

"Not only did you give her children the right color of blankets, for her girls, they were also the right size for their beds."

The Lord works in mysterious ways, bringing comfort to his children.

Jill Ammon Vanderwood is the mother of four grown children and grandmother of six. Jill is the author of three published children's books: Through the Rug, and Through the Rug2: Follow that Dog, and The San Francisco Adventures of Sara The Pineapple Cat, available on Amazon.com. www.throughtherug.com

Jill has been awarded the 2008 League of Utah Writer's Writer of the Year

The Neighbor Dog

By Jill Ammon Vanderwood

In the 1970's my small family lived in Lansdowne, Pennsylvania, along what looked like a lazy country lane. It seemed an ideal place to live and raise two young daughters, across the street from a tree lined park.

Our rental house was a 100-year-old, duplex, seated right on the side of the twisting road. Scottsdale Road was anything but lazy. Motorists took this road as a shortcut, and weren't likely to slow down. There wasn't a sidewalk or a curb, in front of our home. If we stepped off our narrow front porch, we were in the road.

Four other houses also sat next to the road, and behind these run-down homes, up on a grassy hill, was an exclusive, high-rise apartment building. Across the street, the shaded park was inviting during the day time, with the swings, a slide, picnic tables, and the sound of water, rushing down the creek.

I was five months pregnant with my third child. Since the car, parked in our parking strip across the street, wouldn't run, I had the habit of walking to the store, and anywhere else I had to go.

One day, I needed to make a run to the store for bread and milk. My husband, Don, was home, so it was easier to leave him with two-year-old Stephanie and one-year-old Nadean. I climbed the hill behind the house, and crossed the railroad tracks, to get to the store. I stopped to visit my mother's house on the way back, so Mom could give me a ride home. My mother wasn't home that day. I waited, watching TV with my teenage brother and two sisters, as long as I could, before heading back home. But, being so pregnant and realizing that it was getting dark, I headed down Scottsdale Road, in semi-darkness. It got darker the further I went, especially with the cover of trees. After I passed a garden store, I knew there wouldn't be houses for the next half mile. There was no use going inside the store to call home, because we didn't have a telephone.

Every step I took became more ominous. I hadn't gone much further, when I was literally filled with terror. Some unknown danger was waiting down the road for me, and I didn't want to find out. I stopped on the side of the road, before reaching the park. I thought if I go back up the road and take another route, it will be totally dark. If I continue this way, I am sure to come into danger. My unborn son kicked inside me. I lightly stroked my protruding belly, put my hands over my face, while shaking in my shoes, and began to pray. "Heavenly Father, it's getting dark, and I need to get home, I am afraid that there is danger in the park ahead. Please tell me what I should do. Please help me to get home safely"

I heard the sound of clicking on the pavement, behind me. It came closer and closer, as I tentatively continued walking along the road. When the sound came closer, I heard panting, and in the dim light, I saw a large dog bounding toward me. I wondered, is this the danger I was feeling? Is this dog going to harm me? In the dim light, I saw that the dog was a gold-and-white collie. He stopped when he caught up to me.

"Shoo, Shoo, dog!" I demanded, stomping my foot, and waving the jug of milk at him. "Go home, boy, go home, now!" I shouted. The dog didn't leave. When I walked, he walked. When I stopped, he stopped. My fear began to melt away. I continued home, past the darkened outline of swings, teeter-totters and slide. Cars came down the road, with headlights shining on the dog and me. When I reached my house, we crossed the road together. Once again I said, "Shoo, dog, go home!!" He did not leave. I went inside and the dog curled up on the porch. My two little girls hugged the dog. My husband brought out a bowel of water, and we fed him table scraps. Our new protector slept on our porch and he was still there in the morning.

Several evenings each week, we visited the neighbors, who lived a few houses down, to share a meal and play cards, while our children played together. The dog followed us over, and slept on their porch. When we headed home, he stayed on their porch, for the night. He remained on the neighbor's porch for a few days, and then we would find him back on our porch. This continued for about a month. We named him Goldy, then Sonny, but those names didn't seem to fit. While talking with the couple down the road, we all decided to call him 'Neighbor'. He really was a neighbor dog, looking after all of us, on Scottsdale Road.

One morning my little girls ran to see if 'Neighbor' was on our porch, and he wasn't. When we visited our friends down the road, we also found that he wasn't there. "I thought he was at your house," they said.

Our beloved 'Neighbor' dog was gone, as suddenly as he appeared. We missed the dog, which came to help me, one dark and spooky night, on Scottsdale Road, but we were happy to know that our Heavenly Father sends his angels to watch over us, even in the form of a friendly "Neighbor' dog.

Two Seats To Fill

By Kathie M. Thomas

Sometimes it's not always evident a God-incident has happened, until you have all the pieces of the puzzle together. In 2005 Graham and I had an experience that until after the event, wasn't evident it was another God-incident.

I listen to our local Christian radio station, LightFM, every single day. It's on in the background with music playing, voices talking and has a positive input into my life as I work in my office, read, do housework, or whatever. I like having that background sound - it's not intrusive but comforting. I very much enjoy being on my own whilst working but I don't like total silence and the radio station fills that void.

Anyway, LightFM is a listener supported station; very dependent upon donations and sponsors to keep it running as their paid advertising mostly helps pay the staff. So LightFM was advertising its inaugural Fundraising Dinner and I first saw it advertised in their newsletter 'Light Reading'. I was going to ring and book straight away, but it mentioned going in groups if possible; they wanted to fill tables of 10. So I contacted my church by email instead to find out if anyone else was going so we could be on a table with others from our church.

I was pleasantly surprised with a return email from our Pastor's secretary a short time later saying he would like us to be his guests. We felt this to be an honor as we had only been there a year and were still getting to know people within this very large congregation. We also knew that our Pastor would have many others he knew well in the church, so to ask us to join his table seemed very special indeed. Naturally we accepted.

The event took place and was great fun with lots of entertainment and humor, silent auctions and other things. A very good night.

At the end of the evening Ps Rob was saying goodbye to us when he shared it had been very timely to receive my email about the dinner (it had been forwarded to him by someone in the church office). Apparently he had 2 seats left to fill on his table and was wondering who he would offer them to when my email arrived.

Coincidence? No way, God is into building relationships and I'm very aware of that!

We're on duty for God 24/7

By Kathie M. Thomas

Throughout 2007 I'd been working on a new book based on The Proverbs 31 Woman. The book is called "Worth More Than Rubies: The Value of a Work At Home Mum". The journey I'd been experiencing during this time had been amazing and the evidence that God continues to work through things I do will never cease to surprise me. The following is just one such incident.

The most awesome thing happened and I want to share it with you.

Around the time my book was being printed I was annoyed to receive yet another email newsletter from some group I'd never heard of. Because they were obviously Australian, and bearing in mind the spam legislation here, I emailed them and asked how I got on the list - to give them the benefit of the doubt.

The guy answered the same day and advised I'd signed up for their regular newsletter last December and this was a special one-off. I emailed back and suggested that they advise who the 'parent group' is so that recipients know who the sender really is. He responded and agreed, and then he emailed me again:

Kathie, you're a Believer! So am I!!
I just clicked on your link for http://worth-more-than-rubies.com/
Where do you fellowship?

He'd seen the link for my new book in my signature block and followed it and knew instantly where my heart lay.

We ended up emailing back and forth and it turned out that 3 years prior he and his wife were touched by a special ministry that operates from my church. More than that, his wife works at home but is struggling, and none of their friends can relate as they are not in a similar position. He asked if I would consider chatting with her on the phone to encourage her and of course I said yes.

It is important that we always respond to things in a way that is not seen as rude or in bad character at any time. We never know who we are connecting with and the internet allows us to connect with anyone and everyone at any given time. We are on duty, God's duty 24/7.

If I had not responded 'nicely' it's possible we would not have discovered what I now believe to be a 'God-connection' and it thrills me that once again, my Lord is using me to help others.

Section Seven

God and Relationships

1 Peter 1:22 *"Now that you have purified yourselves by obeying the truth so that you have sincere love for each other, love one another deeply, from the heart."*

When Things Go Missing

By Brenda Ivie

As my maternal grandmother aged, she began to have some minor memory loss problems. On returning home to Oklahoma from Texas for Thanksgiving, where we had spent the night with my grandmother, we found the telephone ringing as we opened the door. It was my brother.

"I just thought I'd let you know that you are on Granny's list."

If one of her children, or grandchildren, did something that she disapproved of, that person went on the "Crap List". You stayed on the 'list', until you straightened up, redeemed yourself, or she chose to forgive you.

"What did I do?" I asked, searching my brain to identify anything I might have said or done to offend.

"Well, after you and Tommy left, she tried to find some money and a pistol that she had hidden in her house and it was gone." he replied.

"I didn't take it, and I know Tommy didn't either." I said.

"Everyone knows that," he said," but they can't convince her that she has just misplaced it."

"She had taken all her savings out of the bank, $1,500, and she won't tell anyone where she got the gun. Aunt Mae and Aunt Bid are searching her house as we speak, so maybe they'll find it."

"Okay, let me know if they do."

"I will."

After hanging up the telephone beside our bed, I knelt there and said, "Lord Jesus, you know that I didn't steal from my grandmother, and you know that Tommy didn't either. I don't know where that money and gun are, Lord, but you do, please find it for me and return it to her. And Lord, I know that she is old, so please don't let her die with this black cloud standing between us."

When I got up from my knees, I forgot about the whole incident. So when my brother called me three months later and said, "Well, you're off the 'list'", I asked, "What list?"

"Granny's crap list, you're off of it now."

"OHH!" I said, "so, where did they find it?"

"You know, it was really the strangest thing. Granny was sleeping and she had a dream about where her money and gun were. She woke up and walked right to them and got them. They were in one of those big drawers in her bathroom where she stores her extra sheets. What's really weird is that Aunt Mae and Aunt Bid took out every sheet in that drawer shook them out then refolded them and put them back, and there was nothing in there at all."

When we hung up, I once again knelt by my bed and said, "Thank you, Jesus for your help."

Through A Dream

By Debbie Stevens

The place was my home, a suburb of Sydney. It was winter, the year was 2000.

While my city was celebrating the wonder of our first Olympic games, my life was about to change, forever. I was asleep, and had entered the dream world. Here I was, strolling beside the sea-side, water so blue and crystal-clear, the sand beneath my feet soft as silk and so white that it was almost blinding. There was no other soul on the beach, but suddenly I was aware of a presence walking beside me, speaking words of comfort, reassurance. I couldn't see the face, but I immediately recognized the person. His gown was almost as white as the sand that we walked upon, it felt like time had stopped.

Just as clear as this picture was, so too the feeling of a tap on my shoulder. The kind of tapping as if someone were trying to get my attention, and I awoke. Looking around the bedroom, I expected to wake with either my husband, or one of my children needing me... everyone lay fast asleep.

The next morning, I gathered the family, describing the dream, and the sensation of the hand on my shoulder...no one could explain it so I tried to put it out of my mind.

The following day brought my answer. My mother, who had been fighting a battle with cancer, had fallen during the night... my father found her the next morning.

As I drove my car recklessly up the motorway to her house, I realized in an instant my dream had been a message, a warning. I will always believe that the dream along with the hand that woke me, were both letting me know...'Get ready'

"Side by Side" poem written by Debbie Stevens, is based upon this incident.

Debbie Stevens *has always a lover of poetry and writing since childhood, always encouraged by her mother. The same 'army of words' would come to her rescue shortly after her mother's death; they continue today.*

Blind Date

By Brenda Ivie

In September of 1975, while working as a night shift cook in a local truck stop, one of the waitresses came to me one night and asked if I would be interested in going out with her, her husband and his employer on a 'blind' date. She then began to tell me all the general things that one would tell you about your date-to-be. You know... like, "He's a nice, (funny, cute, sweet, etc.) guy. He has a good job. He has a nice car." Yada, yada, yada...

Yet as she was talking I heard a distinct, very emphatic voice in my mind that said, "Well, I'll end up married to him." This took me totally by surprise, as I had vowed never to marry and had remained unattached. Being twenty-two years old at the time, my mother was convinced I'd be an 'old maid'.

I did go on the blind date, and Tommy was everything that my waitress friend had described.

The next day I saw him and some friends in his car in the grocery store parking lot. I stopped to say hello, and while I squatted by his door talking to him, he suddenly looked into my eyes said, "Will you marry me?" In less than a heartbeat I said yes. All his friends began to tease him, saying "Oh man, you asked the wrong one this time. She said yes." Nothing more was said, and I left to go to work.

We went out on a couple of more dates that weekend, then he had to go to Fort Worth, Texas to sell a load of hay, and was gone for six days. When he returned, he called me for another date. I arrived at the home of some of our mutual friends where he was waiting for me. A few minutes later he asked to see me in to the kitchen. We sat at the table and he asked, "Do you remember, last week when I asked you to marry me?"

"Yes," I replied.

"Well…" he said slowly, "I meant it."

"That's good, " I smiled, "because I meant it when I said yes."

"When do you want to get married?" he asked.

"Well, June is traditional."

"Okay, what day?"

"How about the 25th?"

"All right."

He had to leave for Texas again the following day. Three days later, he returned and we went out together again.

"Brenda," he said, "I can't wait until June to get married."

"So... when do you want to get married?"

"How about next month, on the 25th?"

So we were married on October 25, 1975, a little over one month from the day we met on our blind date. That was almost 33 years ago. We have remained married and have never had a fight, although when we tell anyone that they don't believe it, until they are around us for awhile.

When God brought us together we weren't Christians, but He had His hands on us and knew that we were supposed to be together. We are blessed and we know it, and we are Christians now.

Coincidence or God-incidence?

By Kathy Carlton Willis

Have you ever had a divine appointment, and knew 100 percent for sure that God's hand was on the situation? I've had several of those in my lifetime, and each time, I am amazed by the power of God. Let me give you an example. I asked a friend to add an e-mail link to my online blog, so that readers could contact me. During the same moments she was setting it up, an old friend of mine stumbled across my blog using a search engine. Not knowing how to contact me, he left a comment on the site, from David R. I read the comment and my heart pounded with excitement. I couldn't help but wonder if this was a childhood friend of mine.

Confirmation came in the form of an e-mail from David Rubemeyer, within minutes of when Carmen placed the e-mail link on my site. I'm not sure what made me want to place the link on that day. We had been toying with the idea for a month or so. And who knows why Carmen found time at that exact moment to add the link. But the end result was the reunion of two childhood friends — a brother was found!

It wasn't a coincidence for each of those elements to be in play that day. Who can orchestrate a man to check out a blog, a woman to request an e-mail link, and another woman to add that link, all within minutes of each other? Only God. This was a God-incidence.

That same God sent Philip along the path of the Ethiopian Eunuch at the very time the eunuch was attempting to understand scripture. It was no coincidence for Philip to be at the right place at the right time, it was a God-arranged divine appointment.

I read a quote that said, "One more coincidence, and I'm going to have to believe that God is in control!" I like that. I'm not saying every traffic light, every weed that pops up in a yard, and every paper cut I get are preordained by God to take place. He allows certain things because there is order in this world. But there are times He says, "I'm not just going to allow the normal order, I'm going to step in and cause a certain situation." That is a divine appointment.

I'm glad to know God didn't just create the universe and then sit back and watch how it turns out. He intervenes and participates in our lives in an intimate way. Look for Him today.

Kathy Carlton Willis *gets to fiddle with words for a living. She owns a communications firm and also works alongside husband Russ in ministry. Words are such a powerful thing, a true gift from the Word made flesh. You may contact her at willisway@aol.com or read more at: http://www.kathycarltonwillis.com/*

Choosing Your Life Partner

By Kathie M. Thomas

When I was 32 years of age, a single mum with three small daughters having escaped a difficult marriage that was threatening to become violent, I was working in a government position and attending church regularly. One day a woman at the church came up to me and told me I should be ashamed of myself - throwing my marriage away. Turned out she'd been praying for a husband and desperately wanted to be married.

I spoke with the Pastor who, in turn, told me I was a woman who should be married and needed to pray about it. Me, I'd had enough and wanted to stay single and bring my girls up on my own. I had made a mess of things in that area and didn't feel like trying again.

About a week later a girlfriend at work told me of the criteria she had for meeting guys - five points. I told her I thought that was a rather cold way of approaching things and she said it was her life and she wanted to make sure when she met 'him' he was the right guy. Why waste time on anything less? I began to wonder if God had a message for me and taking Sue's five points I increased them to twelve and prayed over them, at first somewhat cynically, but over time, more in earnest. (Note from author: the points are irrelevant – they could be whatever is important to you in a spouse)

During this period of time one of my associates at our work prayer group told me about a man whose marriage had recently broken up and there were two little girls involved. He asked if we could pray for this man and his family and that God would enter into the situation. At that time I'd been learning about how, if we concentrate on other people and their needs, that God would also look after our needs. So, for a couple of months I was praying over my situation and praying for this man and his situation.

I won't make this a long story but suffice for you to know the man I was praying for ended up asking me out and within one month of getting to know him, he met eleven out of the twelve criteria I'd set - think God had plans for me! Graham soon met that twelfth point as well and in 1991 we married and combined our family of five girls. A coincidence? I don't think so!

Wedding Plans

By Glynis Becker

Ryan and I met at church in June of 1997. Six months later he proposed and I accepted. We were excited to set a wedding date, but realizing that we hadn't known each other very long, we decided to wait until at least the fall of 1998. For years I had dreamed of a fall wedding, in September. September was the perfect month in my opinion: the heat of August wanes and the snow that sometimes shows up in the Midwest in October isn't a threat yet.

However, our church had started a renovation of the sanctuary which wouldn't be done until October. Neither of us could even imagine getting married anywhere else. Additionally, we wanted as many of our extended family members to be in attendance as possible, so we had to plan a time when our family from all over the country could join us. It seemed nearly impossible to find a time that would work for everyone.

Ryan then reminded me that all of his relatives would be coming to South Dakota, like they do every year, for pheasant hunting season in mid-October. The sanctuary would be finished by then, so it was really a perfect choice.

I prayed about it, but I still balked at the idea. I didn't WANT to get married in October. I didn't WANT to celebrate my wedding anniversary every year during hunting season. I didn't WANT what I didn't WANT! Even though I was an emotional bride-to-be, my rational, logical personality took over and I realized that I would have to put away my desire for a September wedding and that the important part was not the date, but the wedding itself. We were going to do this God's way and it seemed that He had decided on October.

We made our plans. I found the dress, did the invitations, bought flowers and dresses for the bridesmaids.

Everything came together well until two weeks before the wedding. Ryan was playing church-league basketball and ruptured a ligament in his knee. I could NOT believe this. "God, what were you thinking?"

If we'd gotten married in September like I wanted, we would already be married and wouldn't have to wonder if Ryan was going to limp down the aisle on crutches or have to have surgery before the big day. I was mad and frustrated, but I was not in control, so I turned it over to God.

"Okay, Lord, I'm trusting in You to make this work."

Then the day came when we would pick my grandmother up from the airport. I saw her get off the plane and almost burst into tears. She was frail and so old-looking, I couldn't believe it. We all knew she had to be sick, but she'd never said anything to us. She did make it to the wedding, but not for the photos beforehand. She came to the reception but didn't stay long.

While we were away on our honeymoon, my mother took her to the doctor and they discovered colon cancer. It was then that I knew that having a wedding in October was no coincidence. God had planned it perfectly. If we had gotten married in September she would not have been as sick and we might have sent her home without taking her to the doctor. God scheduled our wedding so that we could get her the treatment she would not have gotten herself and He rewarded us with another three years with a wonderful lady.

Praise God that He takes such loving care with the lives of His children and shows Himself so freely to those with eyes to see it.

Glynis Becker is a writer living with her husband, Ryan, and their two children in the beautiful Black Hills of south Dakota. She divides her time between working, church activities and volunteering with a local community help agency.

Be Still and Know That I Am God

By Kathie M. Thomas

I was working in a wonderful position, with a Christian boss. I'd had more children and they were growing up, and I'd returned to work to help pay the bills.

I was going through great growth at that time, learning much from my discussions with my boss, and I'd even joined his church. The children and I went to his family's place for meals; I enjoyed being with him and his wife as much as possible.

I still attended my church too (one in the morning, one at night) and during that time I'd become friendly with a lady named Betty, who was my 'elder'. One Sunday morning, Betty took ill during the church service and was rushed to hospital. She appeared to have had a stroke. She returned home around ten days later.

At my work for several days, the words 'Be Still and Know that I am God' kept running around in my head, plus 'Ring Betty'. I dismissed it as fanciful thinking for a few days, until it started to drive me crazy. I couldn't shake the words from my head.

Finally, shaking, I gave in to it and decided to give Betty a ring and see how she was. I wasn't sure how I was going to approach the subject but knew I had to tell her. I plucked up the courage after about five minutes of conversation and told her that I had to say something to her, but didn't know if it were relevant to her. I quoted the verse and stopped.

She was silent at the other end and I wasn't sure if she was still there. I waited. Then she spoke. "It's funny", she said, "but that's what they were telling us about on the Friday night at the elder's meeting before the Sunday I took ill. I dismissed it as not being for me. Whilst I was in hospital they did lots of tests but they could find nothing wrong. They let me come back home but I was still very tired and needing rest. I started to spend time with the Lord and reading His Word. You are right; it's what I needed to hear."

I said my goodbyes to her, my heart gladdened because I had listened and obeyed. But boy, was I shaking!

Section Eight

God and Travel Protection

Psalm 5:11 *"But let all who take refuge in you be glad; let them ever sing for joy. Spread your protection over them, that those who love your name may rejoice in you."*

God-incidence - It's good to talk!

By Carole Williams, Easter 2006

So, celebrating this Easter tide I was musing over the amount of God-incidences in my life over this last short period. I guess many people would call them coincidences. However, I know through very personal experience that God is working in my life all year, not just at Easter.

I was reflecting on my way to the airport to meet a friend at 4.30 a.m. I know, consider it an ungodly hour if you like! I was thinking about business and having one of those time out reflective, holiday thinking periods with nothing better to do than watch the amazing moonset at that time in the morning. I think that was what got me thinking about all the God-incidences that had occurred relating to my business this year. Just looking at what a wonderful world He created.

So, I arrived at the airport and wandered in about 6.45 ah, great! I thought, just time for a nice cup of coffee, before my friend's flight landed. I had been praying about my business on the way up in the car, that God would show me a new direction.

A SERIES OF GOD-INCIDENCE STORIES

Anyway, there I was in the coffee queue smiling and happy, feeling on top of the world. There was a lady standing next to me, she seemed very 'present' and she said, "it's been quite a morning". There began a conversation in the queue which was to last for the next hour. She introduced herself by name, asked if she could join me and we had the most delightful hour, she walked me to the barrier as we continued to talk and she stood with me until my friend came through from the plane.

She was charming, animated, interesting, and lively, had some great stories, a joke and what's more had a small degree of crossover into my own business. Her name was Claire and she was older than me and I think I would probably have a run for my money to keep up with just how much she does in her life, and I have a seven year old to run after.

Anyway, we exchanged email addresses and I passed her a couple of leaflets which I had with me, always good to take your information with you wherever you go and even at holiday times. I sent Claire an email on my return to say how delightful it was to meet her and that it would be great to keep in touch.

I received a prompt reply, saying that she had met another lady in the airport, same day, who also worked with troubled young people and she had passed one of my leaflets to her and she gave me the other person's email address saying that she had told her all about me.

I have no idea where this will all lead but I know that it will not be the last of it! More later. It is amazing how God networks people.

What I should also tell you was that before going into the coffee lounge, I stood feeling a bit vacant for a few minutes before walking over to a newsstand. Now, I never read newspapers as a rule, too much bad news in them. I found myself walking all round the newsstand reading the headlines. As I did, I asked myself "What are you doing here? Why are you reading the headlines, you don't read papers"? Then I walked over to the coffee lounge and stood in the queue. If I had not done that, I would never have met Claire and had the amazing chat and network link that we did. It was an appointment arranged by God, I have those happen all the time and so I say to you all Happy Easter!

He has risen, just as he said. Matthew 28:6

Carole Williams has a background in Training and Life Coaching and is currently working in Education and youth settings. She believes that everyone has God-given talent and huge potential, which they are often afraid to ignite, fearing change. Carole has a desire to see communities transformed through Gods love!

Another Story

By Shelley Marshall

A call from a fan, Cindy, came in today from West Virginia. What a doll she is. The excitement in her voice made me really appreciate the gift God has given me to write the books people like Cindy read. This beautiful young woman invited me to help their young people's group celebrate their third anniversary. Because the group was named after my second book, Young, Sober, & Free, Cindy thought she would ask if I could attend.

This is the trippy part. It just so happens that I am scheduled to be in West Virginia, not 50 miles from her group, around the date of the group's anniversary! If I just move my flight up by a few days I can make it. Now, what are the odds of my schedule just happening to coincide with their anniversary? Pretty good I say, when one believes in God-incidences.

What about you? What God-incidences have happened to you lately? Some say that "coincidence" is the word God uses when He wants to be anonymous. But He cannot fool me! I see my Higher Power behind all the serendipitous events of my life. Where do you see God in your life?

Shelley Marshall has dedicated her life to working with young recovering addicts and their parents. *Her books* Day By Day, Young, Sober, & Free, *and the* Pocket Sponsor *are recovery classics. Her contributions continue to be significant as an author, international trainer and keynote speaker, and researcher in treatment and recovery.*

You can find Shelley at www.Day-By-Day.org

Washed out But Not Washed Up

By Lynne Churchyard

I am a writer, and writers need to do research, sometimes very in-depth research, in the process of writing a book.

I handed my ticket to the uniformed crewmember checking names on his list, I grinned at him like an idiot. He just looked at me and smiled knowingly.

Apparently, he was quite used to idiots making their first trip on the Indian Pacific. Finances didn't stretch as far as a first-class sleeper, so I opted for a Red Kangaroo Class day/night seat that reclined – in a manner of speaking.

The trip was going to take three days from East to West across the continent of Australia.

We were not quite halfway along the journey when I began to suspect something was wrong. The crew stood in small groups talking in hushed tones and then we were asked to assemble in the dining car where someone announced that the train tracks had been washed away on the Nullarbor.

This was the first time it had ever happened. Oh, the tracks had been flooded previously yes,

142

but never washed away. Our journey ended in Adelaide, while Great Southern Railways organized free flights back to Sydney the next day and a complimentary motel stay.

I arrived home bitterly disappointed, knowing I would probably never be able to afford another trip. Yet the train crew had been marvelous in the face of complaints and in some cases, abuse from some of the passengers.

I wrote to Great Southern Railway and told them how much I appreciated all the crew had done to ease the disappointment of the aborted trip.

Two weeks later, a voucher arrived in the mail for a fifty percent discount on a first-class trip on the Indian Pacific. Next time, I would be traveling by first class sleeper.

Lynne Churchyard (2008): Writing has always been a part of my life, I've been published in a Science Fiction Magazine, and several short stories are about to be published in an anthology of short stories. I've recently completed my first book, and continue to write stories, poems and articles for FaithWriters.

Houston, We Have A Problem

By Tammie Trainham

During routine maintenance, water dripped down a line that led to the control panel for the ice plant. Upon hearing a loud pop, the guys ran to the rescue to find flames pouring out of the box. The damage was already done. Kent called an area electrician that we always count on for our bigger projects.

They said that they couldn't fix it this time; it was out of their league. Kent called me and said, "Tammie, this is big and we've gotta pray." You see, we know that nothing is ever out of His league.

Kent called a friend of the family, Tom, who has experience in dealing with this sort of equipment. He, in spite of his health issues, was there to help guide Kent through the clean-up and assessment of the damage. A true God-send.

Later that day while on their way to eat supper at "White's", Tom admitted that they were over his head. He felt that he had proceeded as far as his experience could get them. Kent replied, "Let's sleep on it and see how it looks in the morning."

Well, the night came and went, then there was morning. Tom came by to pick Kent up and head to the ice house.

Upon driving up, they caught a glance of Les at the trailer park rolling up his water line preparing to go home to Amarillo. Kent said, "Tom, would you mind if I asked this guy to take a look at this with us? Les is an electrical engineer." Tom gladly agreed and before they knew it, Les was in the thick of solving the rest of their problems. Another God-send. Not only solving, but he had the skills to make this control panel better than it was before.

You see, last summer on three occasions we had ice jams resulting in busted augers and mountains of ice on the floor. Next week, Les, Tom and Kent will be installing photo eyes, automatic shut-offs and an alert system. This is so far out of our league that we know it is GOD.

God allows trials and tribulations to come because of our disobedience. But in this case, sometimes they just come! And we have to trust that he has a plan to make things better than they were before. Thank you God for coming to our rescue through Tom and Les. Bless these men beyond measure.

Change of Flight Plan

By Pam Archer

It was 1970 and I had flown to Hawaii to meet my husband for R&R. He had been serving in the U.S. Army, in Vietnam. We had a wonderful week there and neither of us wanted to leave. He had to return to Vietnam and I had to fly back to Tennessee.

I was flying on a special military stand-by fare. The night prior to our departure, I received a call from the airline telling me that I had been placed on a later flight, due to my original flight being oversold. "What am I going to do with all this time between you leaving and my flight time?" I cried, as I melted into his arms. I was so sad about being separated and this just added to my distress.

When I returned home on the later flight, I was stunned to see on the news that the flight I initially was scheduled to be on had crashed, killing everyone aboard! I have never questioned a flight change or delay since.

Pam Archer is an author, speaker, columnist, event & wedding planner, fitness pro, and mother of three daughters.

www.pamelaseventdesign.com

Section Nine

God and Work

John 5:17 *"Jesus said to them, "My Father is always at his work to this very day, and I, too, am working."*

You're Allowed To Do Nothing

By Doug Burr

I'm really not much on about things like fortune cookies, etc, but I DO believe God can and DOES speak to us in a myriad ways, including such things now and then. The key is being open and listening to hearing his voice at any time. I mean, he spoke through a donkey to Balaam once!

For example, last year on vacation I opened a "Dove Dark Chocolate Promise" candy, and God used the message on the wrapper to speak to me.

At that time I wasn't sure it was really God, but when I opened another one a day or so later, it had the same message. And because God was "pumping me so hard in the ribs with his elbow," I knew I needed to take the advice he was offering through this particular medium. I might even have blogged about it at the time.

Anyway, with that preamble I'm here to tell you I opened another Dove candy tonight and was almost bowled over with the message:

"You're allowed to do nothing."

Now that probably means nothing to you, but just this morning I said to my wife Debbie: "I'm feeling guilty this year on vacation. Like I shouldn't be just doing nothing."

Now you can take that kind of stuff as coincidence if you'd like. But I don't believe in coincidence - I believe in God-incidence. Either that, or a coincidence is just a time when God chooses to remain anonymous. Take your pick.

This morning in my prayer time, I asked God about my idleness (when we need to be working to win the world) and he told me it was okay to rest. I've always believed that, but for some reason, I'm having trouble shutting things out this year and stopping the mad rush of busy-ness I left back in Maine.

Okay, God - I get it. I heard you and I'll listen. Too bad it took me over a week of vacation to start thinking about stopping.

Tomorrow we've got a few things planned, but I think I might just map out a nice nap on the couch.

Doug Burr, and his wife Debbie, are Pastors with a well-known denomination. Together they have raised two wonderful children who are serving the Lord in their own unique ways.

Answer From God

By Kathie M. Thomas

There was a time when I was working in a bank in South Australia, young, only around 19 years of age.

I loved to wander the main street of the city at lunch times, and it was during this time that a group that claimed to be spiritual soul travelers had set up a tent, to invite in prospective new members. I had begun to visit them, discussing with them my beliefs and the reason why I could not possibly become a part of their group. But their answers confused me and I was unsure.

I went to see a friend who worked nearby and who was a solid Christian. He suggested I pray to God about what He wanted. I prayed that Friday night, that God would show me one way or the other, what He wanted me to do.

On Monday, I was back at my desk and there lay an envelope addressed to me. It seemed a lady from another branch desperately wanted to transfer to town and as I lived near where she was currently working, it had been suggested that I should transfer out there.

I had my answer. I could have argued and said no, I wouldn't go, after all I loved my position, but I did not argue. Because I knew that this was the answer that God had for me and I had to accept it. No more contact with those people!

Coincidence? No, it was a God-incident!

Amazing Direction

By Kathie M. Thomas

I got a phone call from the printer of my BNI (Business Network International) chapter who is only a few minutes drive from me. She had a Pastor in her shop who wanted some typing done, so she sent him to me. Turned out he was one of the Sudanese from Heatherton CRC where my husband and I used to attend for 10 years, and which we had left only a year prior.

He needed a Rules of Association typed for the new Sudanese church being established at Heatherton. He, and the senior pastors there, had been trying to find a copy of this document on the church head office website but it was not there. So he had to find someone to type a copy from the example he had. What are the odds of him going to Highett only to be directed to me? Totally awesome!

Addendum, I should explain that Graham and I shifted to another church because of a direction from God and a change in our Ministry. We loved the years we spent at Heatherton and have many friends there - and a daughter married a son of one of the Pastors from there in 2006.

Section Ten

God and Worship

Psalm 100:2 *"Worship the LORD with gladness; come before him with joyful songs."*

Surprise! God-incidence

By Julia Pferdehirt

A friend once said a new word - God-incidence. Not a chance occurrence. Not "good luck" or even a random act of beauty (and I love random acts of beauty). But one of those God-acts that catches us by surprise. Something we see His hand all over - but usually after the fact.

I had a God-incidence recently. Someone from Care Net (a ministry to people seeking healing from abortion experiences) called my church's office looking for help last fall. Care Net runs a periodic Bible study called 'Forgiven and Set Free' (tuck that bit of information away). At the end of the study, they always invite a pastor to come and read some scripture, say a "few words" and close in prayer.

Now, we've all seen pastors do this (maybe or maybe not with "few" words). The Care Net folks wondered if Faith Community's pastor could come. But we don't have a pastor. Our church is team-led.

Enter the God-incidence. The person who answered the church phone ran upstairs, where I was just finishing a meeting. He said, "there's somebody on the phone and it sounds like you're the person they're looking for."

I picked up the phone. Would I come and do this 'pastor' thing? I would. In fact, tears came.

I had just completed a journey of self-examination using 'The Path', a book by Laurie Beth Jones designed to help you discover and put words to a "personal mission statement". I'd been asking God to show me His purpose and calling for me. I'd asked Jesus to "name" me with His name for me.

The book posed a series of exercises, readings, questions, and both prayer and personal journals leading to a "personal mission statement". The result of mine was "through teaching, encouragement, mentoring, and prayer, offer the healing and wholeness of Jesus to women".

So, armed with an official-sounding personal mission statement, I went out into the world, or at least to another church meeting. Then, Care Net calls.

I ended up doing the "pastor thing" at the Forgiven and Set Free Bible study. Holy Spirit showed me that the women and men needed to be cleansed and blessed. He led me to anoint their minds, hearts and hands with oil, saying "renewed mind, cleansed heart, hand freed to reach out to others". I was afraid people would be offended - knowing what seems normal to me may seem strange or uncomfortable to others. But they weren't. It was beautiful. I was blessed. So were they.

A year later....

God-incidence!

This week I had the privilege of doing the "pastor thing" again at the most recent Forgiven and Set Free study. God kept speaking to me about identity. Saying, forgiveness isn't just something that happens related to a specific sin or problem - in Jesus, forgiveness is who you ARE. Who He makes you by His blood shed for you. You just don't receive forgiveness, you ARE forgiven.

Holy Spirit showed me a sheer, white scarf I'd been given. I was to cover these women and men with this symbol of purity and speak a "new name" - Forgiven.

Again, I was afraid people might be offended. I was afraid they'd be expecting a "pastor" and they'd get me instead. I forgot how God had set this whole thing up a year earlier.

But, my fears were groundless. God-incidence flowed. Nobody seemed to think the "scarf thing" was strange. I was delightfully surprised and blessed. I hope the women and men were as well.

So, sisters. Please tuck the information about the Forgiven and Set Free study in your toolbox. You'll meet someone who needs to search through God's Word to be led to and assured of forgiveness in Jesus.

And, keep your eyes open and your wits about you. God-incidents are everywhere, just waiting for YOU.

Love, Julia

*Author **Julia Pferdehirt** is active in women's ministry in her Madison, Wisconsin home. At present, she's employed part time as pastor of Children's and Family Ministry at Faith Community Bible Church. She's juggling a master's program in Counseling with a new venture – leading healing and recovery groups for women survivors of abuse.*

He Had A Plan

By Laurie Glass

When I look at the poem on my living room wall, it reminds me of how God worked in my life at the time I wrote it. I was shopping for a pretty plaque with a nice saying for my home. But what I found was only appropriate for couples and families, and I am single. I decided to write a poem and frame it. Titled *My Home*, it remains where I first hung it. Little did I know that God would use my writing that poem to usher me into an amazing journey.

Suddenly, my heart swelled and my mind filled with ideas. I HAD to write. As I penned one poem after another, I knew it could only be that God was filling me with His message and using me to put it on paper. I had written poetry off and on for most of my life, but never like that. After writing 30 poems in five weeks, it was clear to me that God was up to something.

Eager to follow God's leading; I began to pray about my writings. I also began to share my poems with others. Their positive feedback surprised and encouraged me. Comments like, "I read your poem every day," and "When I can't sleep, I get up and read your poems," confirmed that God was speaking through me.

In my personal life, I came to the end of my battle with anorexia. After that miracle occurred, I wrote even more. Again, it was as if God filled my heart, and His message flowed through my pen.

God led me step-by-step. One of those steps was joining FaithWriters, a website which provides support, tools and opportunities for Christian writers. With the help and encouragement of the friends I met there, I began to submit my writing for publication.

I have since had several poems and articles published in both print and online publications. I am especially passionate about writing pieces that offer hope and encouragement to those with eating disorders.

I did not plan it, and I did not see it coming. I wrote a poem for myself that was completely unrelated to the writing I do now. But God chose that time to lead me into an amazing writing journey. There is no question in my mind that He wants me to write. And write I will, so He can share His message of hope and healing through me.

Laurie Glass is single, works as a legal assistant/ bookkeeper, holds a degree in Christian counseling and writes on the side. She ministers to others through her writing and her website, Freedom From Eating Disorders www.freedomfromed.com

Contributors

A big thank you to all of those who contributed their stories to this book.

Ps Rob Buckingham

Kathie M. Thomas

Ethel Ashe-Frear

Pam Archer

Glynis Becker

Doug Burr

Janet Camilleri

Shirley Cheng

Lynne Churchyard

Dale H Clifton

Lesley-Anne Evans

Laurie Glass

Lonny J. Gulden

Brenda Ivie

Shelley Marshall

Mavis Matthews

Mulled Vine

Virginia O'Gorman

Julia Pferdehirt

Ian Plumb

Joanne Sher

Debra Shiveley Welch

Debbie Stevens

Christine Thomas

Terri Tiffany

Tammie Trainham

Jill Ammon Vanderwood

Carole Williams

Kathy Carlton Willis

About the Author

Kathie M. Thomas is an Author, Blogger, Speaker and Virtual Assistant Coach & Trainer. She began her business 'A Clayton's Secretary' in 1994 to be home fulltime for her 5 daughters.

Today Kathie runs a global business via the internet from her home office in Melbourne, Australia and her blogging efforts places her in the Top 100 Australian Blogs list. She also contributes to printed and online publications and has published how-to business books.

Her passion is helping women return home to work, using skills they developed in the workforce, so they can be home fulltime for their families. It was because of these community efforts that she was nominated for Australian of the Year in 2008.

Her last book "Worth More Than Rubies: The Value of a Work at Home Mum" achieved #23 in the Top 100 Hot New Releases for her genre during the Amazon.com launch.

Kathie M. Thomas,
PO Box 2918, Cheltenham, Victoria, Australia, 3192
Ph: +613 9585 5780, Fax: +613 9585 3785
kathie@vadirectory.net
www.kathiethomas.com

Quick Order Form

Fax orders: +613 9585 3785

Telephone orders: +613 9585 5780.
Is your credit card ready?

Email or PayPal orders: kathie@vadirectory.net

Postal orders: Kathie Thomas,
PO Box 2918, Cheltenham, Victoria, Australia, 3192

Please send the following books.

It Happened By Design $19.95 _____

Worth More Than Rubies $19.95 _____

How To Become A Virtual Assistant $19.95 _____

From Blog to Book $15.95 _____

Total due: $ _____

Amex / MasterCard / Visa No: _____

Expiry Date: ___/___ Signature: _____

Please send more FREE information on:

❐ Other books   ❐ Speaker/Seminars   ❐ Mailing Lists

Name: _____

Address: _____

City:_____ State: _____ Zip: _____

Telephone (incl country code): _____

Email address:_____

Shipping by air

Australia: $2.00 first book and $1.50 for each book
thereafter

International: $6.50 for first book and $4.00 for each
additional book.
Please allow 6-10 working days for delivery.

www.ingramcontent.com/pod-product-compliance
Lightning Source LLC
Chambersburg PA
CBHW070802100426
42742CB00012B/2222